Adult Daughters of Narcissistic Mothers

Heal Childhood Emotional Neglect, Silence Your Inner Critic, and Feel Confident

Claire Brown

Copyright © 2025 Claire Brown. All rights reserved.

The content of this book may not be reproduced, duplicated, or transmitted without direct written permission from the author or the publisher.

Under no circumstances will any blame or legal responsibility be held against the publisher or author for any damages, reparation, or monetary loss due to the information contained within this book. Either directly or indirectly. You are responsible for your own choices, actions, and results.

Legal Notice:

This book is copyright-protected. This book is only for personal use. You cannot amend, distribute, sell, use, quote, or paraphrase any part or the content within this book without the author's or publisher's consent.

Disclaimer Notice:

Please note the information contained within this document is for educational and entertainment purposes only. All effort has been executed to present accurate, up-to-date, and reliable, complete information. No warranties of any kind are declared or implied. Readers acknowledge that the author is not engaging in the rendering of legal, financial, medical, or professional advice. The content within this book has been derived from various sources. Please consult a licensed professional before attempting any techniques outlined in this book.

By reading this document, the reader agrees that the author is under no circumstances responsible for any losses and/or damages, direct or indirect, incurred as a result of using the information contained within this document, including, but not limited to, errors, omissions, or inaccuracies.

Contents

Introduction	1
Chapter 1	4
Chapter 2	16
Chapter 3	27
Chapter 4	39
Chapter 5	50
Chapter 6	62
Chapter 7	73
Chapter 8	87
Chapter 9	99
Chapter 10	110
Conclusion	122
References	125

Introduction

Julie sat quietly on her couch, the weight of the phone in her hand feeling heavier with every passing second. She had just hung up from another draining conversation with her mother. The familiar sting of criticism lingered in her mind, echoing words she had heard all her life. "Why can't you be more like your sister?" "You're too sensitive." These phrases wrapped around her heart like a vice, tightening with every memory. This was the unending cycle Julie faced as the daughter of a narcissistic mother, an experience all too familiar to many.

This book is for you if you've ever felt trapped in similar patterns. It seeks to help adult daughters of narcissistic mothers heal from the scars of childhood emotional neglect. It will guide you in silencing that relentless inner critic and building a foundation of self-confidence. You deserve to step out of the shadow that has loomed over your life and into your own light.

Within these pages, we will explore several key areas. You will gain a deep understanding of the dynamics in narcissistic relationships and recognize how these dynamics from your childhood seep into your adult life. Most importantly, we will focus on providing effective, real-life solutions for healing and empowerment. This is not about offering vague advice. It's about giving you tools you can use every day.

What sets this book apart is its specific focus on your unique challenges. Many self-help books provide broad advice, but here, you'll find detailed examples that reflect your experiences. The guidance offered is tailored to the reality of daughters with narcissistic mothers. You will find strategies that work specifically for you and your specific circumstances.

Let me speak directly to you, the reader. You are an adult woman who has lived through and managed the complexities of a relationship with a narcissistic mother. You may struggle with self-doubt, fear of criticism, or trouble trusting others. Know that you are not alone. This book recognizes your struggles and speaks to the heart of what you face daily.

As you read, you will gain transformative benefits. You will begin to understand your past and how it has shaped your present. You will learn to reclaim your identity, creating a life that reflects who you truly are. Healthier relationships will become attainable as you learn to set boundaries and communicate effectively.

I invite you to engage fully with this book. Participate in the exercises provided and take actionable steps towards healing. This is not just a passive read; it's an opportunity for you to commit to yourself and start the process of self-discovery and empowerment. Change is possible, and it begins with a single step. It starts now with you reading and absorbing the information in this book.

As you move through these pages, know that you are not alone. This book offers ongoing support and guidance. It provides a sense of community, a place where your experiences are validated and understood. You will find tools to thrive beyond these pages, creating a life of authenticity and joy.

You are capable of breaking free from the past. Let this book be your companion on that journey. Together, we will explore, heal, and grow. You deserve a life filled with confidence and self-assurance. Let's begin.

Chapter 1
Understanding Narcissistic Mothers

You find yourself standing in the kitchen, watching your mother orchestrate another family dinner, her voice soaring over the clatter of dishes. She's recounting tales of your childhood, each story exaggerated to highlight her sacrifices. "I did everything for you," she declares, expecting your nod of gratitude. But beneath the surface, you feel the familiar tug of resentment. Her narrative leaves no room for your own experiences or emotions. It's a scene that plays out in countless homes, leaving daughters feeling unseen. This chapter seeks to unravel the complex matrix of narcissistic motherhood, offering clarity and insight into the dynamics that often leave you questioning your worth.

Defining Narcissism in Mothers

Narcissism in mothers manifests in uniquely insidious ways, distinct from other relationships. A narcissistic mother often cloaks her controlling behavior in the guise of care. On the surface, she may appear attentive, even doting, but this care comes at a cost. Her nurturing is conditional, tethered to her own needs for validation and control. Unlike other forms of narcissism, maternal narcissism is deeply entwined with the life and identity of the child, making it difficult for you to discern where her influence ends and your autonomy begins. This lack of clear boundaries can leave you feeling suffocated and dependent as if your life exists solely to fulfill her needs.

At the core of a narcissistic mother's behavior are traits like grandiosity, entitlement, and a profound lack of empathy. She may perceive her child's achievements as extensions of her own, basking in the reflected glory without acknowledging the child's individuality. This entitlement often leads to a grandiose self-image, where the mother's expectations are set impossibly high, not just for herself but for everyone around her. Manipulative affection becomes another tool in her arsenal, where love and praise are dispensed strategically to maintain control. This manipulation breeds confusion, causing you to question your own feelings and perceptions.

Societal and cultural factors can magnify these traits, adding layers of complexity to the narcissistic dynamic. Cultural notions of maternal sacrifice and the expectation for mothers to appear flawless can exacerbate narcissistic tendencies. A mother may feel immense pressure to present a perfect facade, projecting this expectation onto you. The demands of society for mothers to be selfless saints only serve to validate her manipulative behavior, allowing her to hide behind the guise of cultural norms. This societal reinforcement makes it even more challenging for you to identify and confront the unhealthy patterns in your relationship.

It's important to distinguish narcissistic personality traits from other disorders, such as Borderline Personality Disorder (BPD). While both can involve emotional instability and manipulation, they differ in their underlying motivations and expressions. Narcissistic Personality Disorder (NPD) is characterized by an inflated sense of self and a relentless need for admiration, whereas BPD often involves intense fear of abandonment and unstable interpersonal relationships. Understanding these distinctions is imperative in accurately identifying and addressing the specific behaviors of a narcissistic mother. Recognizing these nuances can empower you to maneuver through your experiences with greater clarity and confidence, creating a path toward healing and self-discovery.

Managing the complexities of a narcissistic mother's behavior requires patience and insight. By understanding the unique characteristics of maternal narcissism and its societal reinforcements, you begin to untangle the intricate web woven around your identity. This knowledge is the first step in reclaiming your sense of self, allowing you to see beyond the distorted reflections imposed upon you. As you dig deeper into these dynamics, remember that your experiences are valid, and your path to healing, though challenging, is one of profound transformation and empowerment.

The Grandiose vs. Vulnerable Narcissist

Understanding the nuances between grandiose and vulnerable narcissistic mothers is crucial for grasping the impact they have on their daughters. Grandiose narcissists exude overt self-importance. They thrive on attention and admiration, often seeking it in public spheres. These mothers may dominate conversations, ensuring all eyes remain on them. Their sense of superiority is palpable, creating an environment where their needs and achievements overshadow everyone else's. In family settings, such a mother might monopolize family gatherings, turning every event into a platform to showcase her achievements and highlight her perceived excellence. Her daughters often feel like supporting characters in their own lives, struggling to be heard or seen amidst the blinding spotlight their mother demands. This constant overshadowing can lead to feelings of inadequacy and emotional neglect, as their own achievements and needs are disregarded.

On the other hand, vulnerable narcissists present a different yet equally challenging dynamic. They are marked by hypersensitivity to criticism and deep-seated insecurity. These mothers might not seek the limelight as overtly as their grandiose counterparts, but their need for validation is just as strong. In family settings, they may exhibit passive-aggressive behaviors, using guilt or emotional withdrawal as a means to manipulate those around them. For example, a vulnerable narcissist might sulk for days after perceiving a minor slight, leaving the daughter to guess what went wrong and how to fix it. This type of emotional manipulation can be subtle yet deeply impactful, fostering a sense of instability and confusion. Daughters of vulnerable narcissists often walk on eggshells, constantly adjusting their behavior to avoid triggering their mother's insecurities.

The impacts on daughters differ significantly between these two narcissistic types. Daughters of grandiose mothers often experience emotional neglect. Their own needs and emotions are sidelined in favor of their mother's grand narrative. This neglect can leave lasting scars, making it difficult for these daughters to assert themselves or recognize their own worth in adulthood. They may struggle with feelings of invisibility, always questioning if their achievements are ever enough. Conversely, daughters of vulnerable narcissists endure emotional manipulation. Their mothers' insecurities and hypersensitivity mean that these daughters become adept at managing and mitigating their mother's emotional states. This hyper-vigilance can lead to anxiety and a skewed sense of responsibility for others' emotions. They may grow up believing they must placate and please to ensure harmony, often at the expense of their own needs.

Consider the story of a woman whose mother was a prominent figure in the local community, a classic example of a grandiose narcissist. Her mother used her public role to reinforce her superiority, often recounting tales of her own successes at every opportunity. Family dinners became performances, with her mother at the center stage, leaving little room for anyone else, including her daughter, to share or be acknowledged. This constant overshadowing left the daughter feeling invisible, her accomplishments always eclipsed by her mother's narratives. On the flip side, imagine another scenario where a daughter's vulnerable narcissist mother would react to perceived slights with days of silent treatment. This passive-aggressive behavior kept the daughter in a state of constant anxiety, always trying to decode her mother's moods and preemptively soothe them. The daughter learned early on to prioritize her mother's emotional state over her own, a pattern that followed her into adult relationships.

Understanding these dynamics is so very important. Recognizing whether your mother exhibited grandiose or vulnerable traits can provide clarity and help as you untangle these complex emotional threads. Each type leaves a distinct imprint, influencing how daughters relate to the world and themselves.

Emotional Manipulation Tactics

In dysfunctional family dynamics, emotional manipulation is a tool wielded with unsettling precision by narcissistic mothers. Narcissistic mothers are masters at using this for their own gain and to the detriment of their daughters. At the forefront of these tactics is gaslighting, a form of psychological manipulation that sows seeds of self-doubt and confusion. Imagine a moment when you recall a conversation about an important decision, only for your mother to insist it never occurred or that you misunderstood. Such denials twist your perception of reality, leaving you questioning your memory and judgment. This tactic erodes your self-esteem, making you reliant on her version of events, ultimately giving her control over your narrative. Triangulation, another insidious tactic, involves your mother pitting family members against each other to maintain dominance. She might praise one sibling while criticizing another, sowing discord and competition. This strategy keeps you off-balance, unsure of who to trust, and often desperate for her approval. The psychological impact of these manipulations is both powerful and lasting. Over time, the constant barrage of doubt and division can lead to anxiety, depression, and a distorted sense of self-worth. You may find yourself seeking validation externally, never trusting your own instincts.

Recognizing and responding to these tactics is crucial for reclaiming your agency. One powerful strategy is journaling. By documenting your experiences and emotions, you create a tangible record that can counteract your mother's attempts to distort reality. Writing down conversations and outcomes provides clarity, helping you see patterns and manipulations more clearly. It can become a tool for validating your feelings and experiences, reinforcing that your perception matters. Consulting with a trusted friend also offers an external perspective, grounding you when doubt creeps in. This friend can act as a sounding board, affirming your experiences and offering insights that may not be apparent when you're caught in the emotional whirlwind.

Consider a scenario where you achieved a significant milestone at work, such as a promotion. Instead of celebrating your success, your mother dismisses it as trivial, saying something like, "Well, it's about time they noticed you." Her words, though masked as encouragement, minimize your achievement, leaving you questioning its worth. This subtle form of manipulation can diminish your joy, making you feel as though nothing you do is ever quite enough. In family gatherings, guilt-tripping is often a favored tactic. Picture a holiday dinner where your mother reminisces about the sacrifices she made for you, strategically emphasizing her struggles to elicit gratitude and guilt. Her narrative might sound like, "If it weren't for me, you wouldn't have what you do today," effectively shifting the focus and creating a sense of indebtedness. This manipulation can feel suffocating, as though you owe your success and happiness to her alone.

To counteract these manipulations, it's healthy to develop strategies that reinforce your autonomy. Setting clear boundaries becomes vital, allowing you to assert your needs and protect your emotional well-being. Practice phrases like, "I appreciate your input, but I've got this under control," to maintain your stance without engaging in conflict. Seeking therapy can also provide a safe space to explore these dynamics and develop coping mechanisms. A therapist can guide you through exercises that strengthen your self-esteem and help you manage the complexities of your relationship with your mother.

Remember, these tactics are not a reflection of your worth or capabilities. They are tools used to exert control and maintain dominance. By recognizing and addressing them, you take the first steps towards regaining your self-confidence and independence. You are not alone in this struggle, and there are paths to healing and empowerment that honor your experiences and foster growth.

The Impact of Narcissistic Parenting on Children

Growing up under the watchful eye of a narcissistic mother casts a long shadow over a daughter's mental health and development. The constant barrage of criticism and manipulation plants deep seeds of self-doubt and insecurity. From a young age, you may have internalized the belief that your worth is inextricably linked to meeting your mother's expectations. This chronic self-doubt becomes a persistent companion, whispering that you are never enough. In situations where you should feel confident, a fear of failure and rejection looms, casting doubt on your abilities. This fear doesn't just hinder your achievements; it shapes your worldview, altering how you perceive challenges and setbacks. No matter how minor, each misstep is magnified, feeding into the narrative that you must be perfect to be loved. This relentless pressure can manifest in anxiety, manifesting in a paralyzing hesitation to take risks or pursue opportunities that could lead to growth.

These early experiences ripple into adulthood, impacting how you form and maintain relationships. Trust, a fundamental component of healthy connections, becomes fraught with difficulty. Having learned that love is conditional, you may find it challenging to trust partners fully, always waiting for the other shoe to drop. This lack of trust can lead to a cycle of sabotage, where the fear of intimacy and vulnerability undermines the potential for genuine connection. Coupled with this, an over-dependence on external validation becomes a coping mechanism. You might find yourself constantly seeking approval from friends, colleagues, or romantic partners, believing that their acceptance is a measure of your worth. This reliance can lead to codependency, where your sense of identity is tethered to the opinions and emotions of others, leaving you vulnerable to manipulation and disappointment.

Struggling with identity and self-worth becomes a central theme in your life. The blurred lines between personal desires and imposed expectations create a confusion that can be hard to handle. Growing up, you might have been praised for achievements that aligned with your mother's narrative, leaving you to wonder what truly matters to you. This lack of clarity fosters an inadequate self-perception, where your achievements never feel like enough, and your failures feel monumental. Your world feels like a constant balancing act, trying to align your genuine self with the version your mother crafted. This internal conflict can lead to feelings of alienation as if you're living someone else's life, and the journey to self-discovery feels like an uphill battle.

Therapists often encounter these patterns in their practice, highlighting the long-lasting impact of narcissistic parenting. They observe that many daughters of narcissistic mothers struggle with self-doubt and identity confusion, often feeling trapped in cycles of people-pleasing and self-criticism. A therapist might note how these women often prioritize the needs of others over their own, fearing rejection if they assert their desires. Personal stories further illuminate this struggle. One woman recalls how her mother's constant comparisons with others left her feeling perpetually inadequate, a sentiment that followed her into her career. Despite achieving professional success, she found herself unable to celebrate her accomplishments, always discounting them as luck or fluke, a testament to the deep-seated impact of her upbringing.

These insights reveal the pervasive nature of narcissistic parenting and its effects, emphasizing the importance of addressing these challenges. Understanding that these patterns are a result of your environment, not your inherent worth, is a crucial step in breaking free from their hold. Recognizing these effects allows you to begin the healing process, providing a sense of empowerment and self-acceptance that can transform your relationships and personal well-being.

Recognizing the Gaslighting Cycle

Gaslighting is a manipulative tactic that distorts reality, making you question your own perceptions and memories. When wielded by a narcissistic mother, it becomes a powerful tool to maintain control. Imagine recounting a family event where you distinctly remember her promising to support your college choice. Later, she denies ever making such a promise, that she never endorsed your choice of college, and insisting that you misunderstood her intentions. This denial of past events is the hallmark of gaslighting, creating a fog around your memories and undermining your confidence in your own reality. Your feelings, no matter how valid, are dismissed, leaving you feeling isolated and confused. This dismissal is not a mere oversight; it is a calculated move to keep you dependent on her narrative.

Understanding the cycle of gaslighting can help you identify it in real time. Initially, your mother may charm you, creating an environment where her affection feels unconditional. This charm lulls you into a sense of security, making the subsequent manipulation harder to detect. Gradually, she introduces doubt, subtly questioning your memory or feelings with phrases like, "Are you sure that's what happened?" or "You're too sensitive." This seeds doubt in your mind, eroding your confidence. Over time, as these seeds take root, your grasp on reality begins to weaken, leaving you reliant on her to interpret events and emotions. This erosion of reality is the gaslighter's ultimate goal, to make you dependent on their perspective.

Breaking free from this cycle requires vigilance and proactive strategies. Keeping a factual journal is a powerful first step. Documenting conversations, promises, and your feelings provides a written record that can counteract her attempts to distort reality. This practice not only reinforces your memory but also validates your experiences. Additionally, seeking validation from outside sources, such as friends or mental health professionals, provides a much-needed perspective. They can offer reassurance and confirm that your experiences are legitimate and not a fabrication of your imagination.

Consider a typical dialogue where gaslighting unfolds. You might remind your mother of a promise she made to help you with a significant purchase. She responds with, "I never agreed to that. You must have imagined it." This interaction leaves you questioning your memory, wondering if you indeed misunderstood. Another scenario might involve her shifting blame onto you during a heated discussion. "I wouldn't have reacted that way if you hadn't provoked me," she might say, effectively deflecting responsibility and making you feel at fault for her behavior. These tactics can trap you in a cycle of self-doubt and guilt, reinforcing your reliance on her version of events.

To counteract these manipulations, it's essential to establish boundaries and reinforce your autonomy. Developing a strong support network of friends or professionals who understand your situation can provide the encouragement needed to stand firm. Practicing assertive communication, where you express your needs and experiences confidently, helps protect your sense of reality. Remember, gaslighting is a reflection of her need for control, not of your inadequacy or failure. By recognizing these tactics and employing strategies to counter them, you reclaim your narrative and reinforce your self-worth.

Recognizing and escaping the gaslighting cycle is not easy, but it is possible. The fog begins to lift as you learn to trust your instincts and validate your own experiences. Your confidence grows, and the terrain of your life shifts from one dominated by doubt to one where your truth shines brightly. Embrace this clarity with courage, knowing that your reality is valid and your voice, once muffled, now has the power to be heard.

Chapter 2
Childhood Experiences and Emotional Scars

Picture a young girl, perhaps no older than eight, standing nervously in the living room as her mother surveys the scene. Her brother, praised for his accomplishments, sits confidently, basking in the warmth of his mother's approval. She, on the other hand, shifts uncomfortably as her mother's gaze turns critical, ready to assign blame for the family's latest mishap. In this household, roles are rigidly defined: he is the golden child, and she is the scapegoat. This dynamic, though unspoken, dictates the rhythm of her childhood, shaping her sense of worth and identity in profound ways.

In the complex ecosystem of a narcissistic family, the golden child and scapegoat serve distinct yet equally damaging purposes. The golden child is lavished with praise and privileges, an extension of the mother's ego, embodying her perceived perfection. This child becomes the pedestal on which the mother displays her triumphs, a living testament to her success as a parent. Meanwhile, the scapegoat absorbs the family's frustrations and failures and is blamed for any disruption or discord. This role provides a convenient outlet for the mother's dissatisfaction, deflecting attention away from her shortcomings. These roles are not static; they may shift or overlap as the mother's whims dictate, but their impact remains deeply entrenched in the household hierarchy.

For the scapegoat, life becomes a relentless struggle against internalized blame and shame. Every misstep, real or imagined, is magnified, reinforcing the narrative that they are inherently flawed. This constant barrage of criticism erodes their self-esteem, leaving them questioning their worth and place in the world. The scapegoat often grows up feeling like an outsider, not only in their family but in broader social circles as well. This perceived inadequacy can lead to a lifelong battle with self-doubt, making it difficult for them to assert their needs or believe in their capabilities. Yet, paradoxically, the scapegoat may also develop resilience and independence, qualities forged in the crucible of adversity. In the absence of familial support, they learn to rely on their inner strength, carving out a path that defies the limitations imposed upon them.

Conversely, the golden child carries the weight of expectation, burdened by the need to maintain their exalted status. The mother's pride in their achievements is conditional, predicated on their continued ability to uphold the façade of perfection. This pressure to constantly perform can create a pervasive fear of failure, leaving the golden child anxious and insecure. Beneath the veneer of success lies a struggle with self-expression, as their true desires and emotions are often suppressed to align with the mother's vision. This internal conflict can manifest in adulthood as difficulties in forming authentic relationships or pursuing passions that deviate from the prescribed path. The golden child may find themselves trapped in a cycle of people-pleasing, driven by an unrelenting need to validate their worth through external accolades.

Consider the story of a scapegoat unjustly punished for a sibling's mistake. When a vase is found broken, and no one admits guilt, the scapegoat is swiftly blamed despite their protests. In the eyes of the mother, their denial is further evidence of their deceitfulness, reinforcing the scapegoat's role as the family's perennial culprit. This incident, though seemingly trivial, leaves a lasting imprint, teaching the scapegoat that truth is often irrelevant in the face of predetermined bias. On the other hand, envision a golden child receiving excessive praise for a talent show performance. Their mother beams with pride, recounting the event to anyone who will listen, amplifying the child's accomplishments to reflect her own glory. This adoration feels intoxicating yet precarious, as the golden child knows that a single misstep could topple their status. Such scenarios illustrate the insidious nature of these roles, embedding themselves in the family's fabric and dictating the emotional landscape of its members.

Understanding these dynamics is crucial for recognizing the hidden scars that shape your adult life. Whether you identify with the scapegoat or the golden child, the psychological impact is undeniable, influencing how you handle relationships and perceive yourself.

Emotional Neglect and Its Lifelong Effects

Growing up with a narcissistic mother often means finding yourself alone in a crowded room. Emotional neglect, in this context, isn't about absence. It's about being invisible despite her presence. A narcissistic mother may be physically there, managing the household or attending school events, but emotionally, she's miles away. Her indifference to your feelings is palpable. She might dismiss your fears as trivial or your joys as unimportant, leaving you to navigate your emotional world without guidance. This lack of support creates a chasm, a void where nurturing should be, forcing you to suppress your needs to avoid being a burden. This emotional void isn't just a gap; it's a canyon that shapes your understanding of love and acceptance.

The effects of such neglect ripple far into adulthood, casting shadows over your relationships and self-esteem. You may find it challenging to express emotions, as years of invalidation taught you to bury them deep. This suppression can manifest as chronic feelings of emptiness, a gnawing sensation that something vital is missing. In relationships, this void can lead to an inability to form deep connections. You might shy away from intimacy, fearing vulnerability or rejection. The habit of self-neglect becomes ingrained, making it difficult to identify or articulate your desires to others. This can leave you feeling disconnected from others and yourself as if living behind a facade that conceals your true self.

Recognizing the signs of emotional neglect in your adult life is essential for healing. You may notice a pattern of trouble forming deep connections, where friendships feel superficial or transactional. There's an inability to pinpoint what truly brings you joy or fulfillment, as your needs were often overshadowed by your mother's. This disconnect manifests as a struggle to assert your identity, leading to an overreliance on others for validation. Understanding these patterns is the first step towards breaking them. Acknowledge that these behaviors are remnants of your past, not reflections of your worth. This awareness can be liberating, providing a foundation for growth and change.

Healing from emotional neglect is a journey of self-compassion and exploration. Begin by practicing self-compassion. Acknowledge your feelings without judgment, recognizing that they are valid and deserve attention. Allow yourself to feel without the fear of being dismissed. Engaging in therapy can also provide a safe space to explore these deep-seated wounds. A therapist can guide you through emotional exploration, helping you uncover and process the neglected parts of yourself. This professional support can be transformative, offering tools to rebuild your self-esteem and redefine your relationships. Therapy becomes a mirror, reflecting your inner world and enabling you to see yourself clearly and kindly.

Incorporate reflection exercises into your routine to help develop self-awareness. Consider journaling your emotions daily and observing patterns without judgment. Let this practice be a safe place for you where your thoughts are free to flow, unencumbered by external expectations. Over time, these reflections may reveal hidden desires and unmet needs, guiding you toward authentic self-expression. As you progress, celebrate small victories, whether it's expressing a previously suppressed emotion or asserting a boundary. These milestones are not mere steps but leaps toward reclaiming your emotional landscape. This journey requires patience and perseverance, yet each step taken is a testament to your resilience and capacity for growth.

The Burden of Perfectionism

In the household of a narcissistic mother, perfection isn't just encouraged; it's demanded. High expectations loom over every aspect of life, and criticism waits eagerly in the wings. As a daughter, you may have been tasked with embodying your mother's unattainable ideals, each achievement scrutinized, every flaw amplified. The drive for perfection becomes a survival mechanism, a way to earn praise instead of critique. But this relentless pursuit isn't born from a desire to excel; it's a defense against the sting of her disappointment. Over time, striving for flawlessness transforms from an expectation into an internalized burden, one you carry into adulthood, even as it weighs heavily on your spirit.

This quest for perfection takes a significant toll on mental health. Anxiety becomes a constant companion, whispering doubts and fears at every turn. The pressure to meet impossible standards can lead to burnout as you push yourself beyond reasonable limits in a desperate bid for approval. In the shadow of potential failure, inadequacy festers, feeding a fear that undermines confidence and stifles growth. The perfectionist mindset traps you in a cycle of self-criticism and worry, where nothing ever feels good enough. This fear of falling short seeps into every corner of life, creating a barrier between where you are and where you hope to be.

Perfectionism doesn't just hinder mental well-being; it actively sabotages personal and professional endeavors. The fear of not meeting standards leads to procrastination, an ironic twist where the need for perfection results in paralysis. You put off tasks, fearing failure if you don't perform flawlessly, and the delay only adds to the pressure. In relationships, the same fear can prevent you from opening up, worried that revealing imperfections might lead to rejection. This need for control limits spontaneity and authenticity, creating a facade that keeps others at arm's length. In the workplace, you might avoid taking risks or pursuing opportunities, worried that any misstep will confirm your worst fears.

To combat perfectionism, it's important to adopt strategies that promote balance and self-compassion. Setting realistic goals is a starting point, allowing you to aim high without the weight of unrealistic expectations. Break tasks into manageable steps, celebrating small victories along the way. This approach not only reduces pressure but also builds confidence, reminding you that progress is possible without perfection. Practicing self-acceptance is equally important. Recognize that mistakes are part of growth, not evidence of failure. Embrace imperfections as learning opportunities rather than shortcomings to hide. Affirmations can serve as powerful reminders, affirming your worth beyond accomplishments.

Consider incorporating mindfulness practices to stay grounded in the present moment. Techniques like meditation or focused breathing can help relieve the cycle of worry, helping you focus on what truly matters. Therapy can also offer valuable support, providing a space to explore the roots of perfectionism and develop healthier coping mechanisms. A therapist can guide you in challenging negative thought patterns, offering tools to reframe your perspective and build self-compassion. Journaling can serve as an additional outlet, allowing you to process emotions and track progress, celebrating growth without judgment. Through these practices, you can gradually release the grip of perfectionism, cultivating a life where authenticity and self-worth thrive without the need for flawlessness.

Isolation and Loneliness in Childhood

Growing up under the influence of a narcissistic mother often means living in a world where isolation is the norm. She expertly crafts a bubble around you, shielding you from external influences that might challenge her control. Friendships that could offer solace and perspective are discouraged or outright sabotaged. Perhaps you remember moments when she belittled your friends, making subtle comments that planted seeds of doubt about their intentions. "Are they really your friends?" she might ask, casting a shadow over relationships that should be sources of joy. Social interactions become fraught with tension, as any bond you form is seen as a threat to her dominance. The result is a childhood spent on the periphery, watching others interact freely while you remain tethered to her expectations.

This forced isolation breeds a profound sense of loneliness and abandonment. You might grow up feeling like an outsider, perpetually disconnected from the vibrant world around you. The belief that you are unlovable takes root, nourished by her indifference to your emotional needs. Dependence on your mother for companionship becomes a survival mechanism, as she becomes the central figure in an otherwise solitary existence. Yet, this dependence is fraught with its own challenges. Her affection is unpredictable, leaving you constantly guessing how to maintain her favor. This uncertainty fosters a deep-seated anxiety as the fear of losing her approval looms ever-present.

As you transition into adulthood, the shadows of childhood isolation linger, casting doubt over your ability to form and maintain meaningful relationships. Trust, already fragile, becomes a scarce commodity. You might find yourself wary of intimacy, hesitant to open up to others for fear of rejection or betrayal. Friendships can feel superficial as if an invisible barrier prevents you from fully engaging with those around you. The skills needed to navigate social situations, skills that are often honed in adolescence, remain underdeveloped, leaving you feeling awkward and unsure in group settings. This hesitance to connect can lead to a self-imposed isolation, mirroring the emotional solitude of your childhood.

Overcoming these feelings of isolation requires intentional effort and a willingness to step beyond the confines of past experiences. Building healthy relationships starts with joining support groups, where you can share your story with others who understand and validate your experiences. These groups provide a safe space for connection, allowing you to practice vulnerability and trust in an environment free from judgment. Open communication is another crucial component in making genuine connections. Start by expressing your feelings and needs honestly with those you trust, gradually expanding your circle of confidants. This openness encourages reciprocal honesty, laying the foundation for deeper, more meaningful relationships.

Engaging in activities that require community involvement can also help bridge the gap left by childhood isolation. Consider volunteering for causes that resonate with your values or joining clubs that align with your interests. These environments offer opportunities to meet others with shared passions, creating a natural platform for connection. As you engage with these communities, practice active listening and empathy, skills that strengthen interpersonal bonds. Remember, building relationships is a gradual process requiring patience and persistence. Celebrate small victories, like attending a social event or initiating a conversation, as these steps mark significant progress in breaking free from the isolation of the past.

Conditional Love and Its Consequences

Surviving a world where love is conditional can leave deep and lasting scars. In narcissistic families, love is often wielded as a tool for manipulation and control. It's a currency, contingent upon obedience, achievements, or meeting the shifting standards set by a narcissistic mother. This kind of love is not freely given; it must be earned, leaving you constantly striving to meet expectations that may never be attainable. The affection you receive feels transient, dependent on your ability to please and perform. This conditional love creates an environment where you learn early on that your value is tied to your accomplishments and compliance rather than your inherent worth.

Growing up with this mindset fundamentally affects your self-worth. The belief that love must be earned becomes ingrained, and you carry it into every aspect of your life. Relationships become transactional, where the fear of rejection looms large. You may find yourself bending over backward to gain approval, terrified that any slip-up will lead to being abandoned or unloved. This internalized belief influences how you perceive yourself and others, leading you to constantly question if you are lovable just as you are. The deep-seated fear of not being enough can lead to anxiety and a persistent need for validation as you seek confirmation from others that you do indeed matter.

The long-term effects of conditional love are profound, shaping how you interact with others and how you see yourself. This upbringing can result in a pattern of over-pleasing, where you prioritize others' needs at the expense of your own. You might find yourself in relationships where your boundaries are consistently pushed, yet you feel powerless to assert them. This tendency to overcompensate stems from a desire to avoid the perceived threat of rejection, which feels ever-present. Your self-perception becomes entangled with how others view you, leading to a cycle of self-neglect and resentment. Over time, this can erode your sense of identity, leaving you feeling lost and disconnected from your true self.

To break free from these patterns, cultivating self-love becomes crucial. Begin by practicing affirmations of self-worth, reminding yourself daily that you are deserving of love and respect, irrespective of your achievements or others' opinions. Affirmations can serve as powerful tools to rewire your thinking, shifting the focus from external validation to internal acceptance. Engage in activities that bring you joy and fulfillment, allowing you to connect with your passions and interests. These pursuits can help reinforce your sense of self, independent of your roles or accomplishments. By prioritizing activities that nourish your soul, you create a space where self-love can flourish, free from the constraints of conditional acceptance.

Incorporate mindfulness practices that encourage self-reflection and emotional awareness. Techniques such as meditation or journaling can help you identify and process emotions that stem from conditional love. This self-awareness is a critical step in recognizing and challenging the beliefs that no longer serve you. Therapy can also offer a supportive environment to explore these dynamics, providing insights and strategies to build healthier relationships with yourself and others. A therapist can guide you to understand and process the complex emotions tied to your upbringing, offering tools to cultivate a sense of unconditional self-worth.

As you work through these challenges, remember that healing is a gradual process requiring patience and persistence. Celebrate small victories, like setting a boundary or expressing a need, as these steps signify progress in reclaiming your autonomy. Each action you take towards self-acceptance is a testament to your resilience and capacity for growth. This chapter has explored the scars left by conditional love, which deeply affect your identity and relationships. As you move forward, the pathway of healing and self-discovery continues, leading you toward understanding, empowerment, and healthier connections.

Chapter 3
Adult Manifestations of Childhood Trauma

Trust is a fragile thing. For daughters of narcissistic mothers, this fragility is often rooted in childhood experiences marked by manipulation and inconsistency. Imagine a young girl eagerly sharing her achievements only to have her mother dismiss her efforts as trivial. This cycle, repeated over years, breeds a deep-seated mistrust. You may have learned early on that expressions of love and approval were often laced with ulterior motives. These experiences teach you to question the sincerity of others as the line between genuine affection and manipulation becomes blurred in your formative years. This fear of betrayal takes root, creating a defensive barrier that follows you into adulthood.

In romantic relationships, these trust issues transform into significant hurdles. The reluctance to open up emotionally stems from the fear of repeating past betrayals. You might find yourself withholding feelings or thoughts, afraid that vulnerability will be met with rejection or ridicule. This emotional armor, while protective, can stifle intimacy and connection, leading to a constant need for reassurance from partners. You seek validation that their affection is genuine, not a precursor to manipulation or deceit. This cycle can be exhausting for both you and your partner as the relationship becomes weighed down by the need for constant affirmation.

The impact of trust issues extends beyond romantic relationships, seeping into friendships and professional interactions. In friendships, you may harbor suspicion of others' motives, questioning whether their intentions are sincere or self-serving. This skepticism makes forming deep connections challenging, as you guard your emotions and thoughts closely. Similarly, in professional settings, trust issues manifest as wariness of colleagues' actions. You might find yourself second-guessing their intentions and interpreting innocent gestures as potential threats. This constant vigilance can create a tense work environment where collaboration feels like a minefield rather than a partnership.

Building trust is a gradual process, requiring patience and intentional effort. Engaging in trust-building exercises can be a valuable step towards fostering healthier relationships. Start small, with achievable trust goals. For instance, practice sharing minor personal details with a trusted friend and observe their response. This exercise helps you gauge sincerity and reinforces that not everyone will use your vulnerability against you. As you grow more comfortable, gradually increase the depth of shared information. Another strategy is to set clear boundaries and communicate them with those around you. This clarity provides a framework within which trust can flourish, as both parties understand and respect each other's limits.

Trust Mapping

Create a trust map to visualize the trust levels in your various relationships. Draw a circle and place your name in the center. Around your name, position the names of people in your life based on how much you trust them. The closer they are to your name, the greater the trust. Reflect on what factors contribute to their placement and consider small actions you can take to move them closer. This exercise encourages reflection on your trust perceptions and helps identify areas for growth.

As you work through these trust challenges, remember that building trust is not about erasing past experiences but creating new patterns supporting healthy relationships. Trust is not built overnight; it is a mosaic of small, consistent actions. Each step you take towards vulnerability is a testament to your courage and resilience, paving the way for deeper, more meaningful connections.

Self-Doubt and the Inner Critic

In the heart of a childhood shaped by narcissistic parenting, self-doubt finds fertile ground. As a daughter, you may have internalized the relentless criticism and high expectations imposed by your mother. Each word, a subtle jab at your abilities, gradually becomes entwined with the core of your self-perception. Over time, this external criticism transforms into an internal monologue, the voice of the inner critic echoing your mother's disapproval. It questions your every decision, painting your achievements in shades of inadequacy. This critic is not an isolated voice; it is the culmination of years of hearing that you were never quite enough. It thrives on your hesitation, growing louder with each perceived mistake until it becomes a constant companion in your mind.

The impact of this self-doubt extends far into your adult life, particularly affecting your ability to make decisions. Faced with trivial or significant choices, you may find yourself paralyzed by the fear of making the wrong move. Your mind races through endless scenarios, each one highlighting potential pitfalls and failures. This overanalysis becomes a barrier, preventing you from taking decisive action. You might spend hours weighing options, only to find yourself stuck in a loop of indecision. The fear is not just about making a mistake; it's about confirming the inner critic's narrative that you're incapable of making the right choice. This paralysis can seep into all aspects of life, from career decisions to personal relationships, leaving you trapped in a cycle of uncertainty.

The inner critic doesn't just halt decision-making; it gnaws away at your self-esteem, creating a destructive cycle of negative self-talk. You might find yourself engaging in self-sabotaging behaviors, consciously or unconsciously undermining your own success. Perhaps you procrastinate on important projects, fearing that any outcome will fall short of perfection. Or you might avoid taking on new challenges, convinced that failure is inevitable. This self-doubt becomes a self-fulfilling prophecy, as the inner critic's harsh judgments erode your confidence and motivation. The more you listen to this critical voice, the more it shapes your identity, convincing you that you're unworthy of success and happiness.

Silencing the inner critic requires intentional effort and self-compassion. One effective technique is practicing positive affirmations. Start each day by affirming your worth and capabilities, countering the inner critic's negativity with statements of self-love and acceptance. These affirmations can gradually help rewire your thought patterns, fostering a more positive self-image.

Cognitive reframing is another powerful tool. This involves challenging negative thoughts and replacing them with more balanced perspectives. When your inner critic whispers that you're destined to fail, counter it by acknowledging past successes and reminding yourself of your strengths. Over time, these techniques can weaken the inner critic's hold, allowing your true voice to emerge.

You might also consider engaging in mindfulness practices, such as meditation or deep breathing exercises, to cultivate awareness of your thoughts. Mindfulness helps you observe the inner critic without attachment, creating space between its judgments and your self-identity. This awareness empowers you to respond with kindness and curiosity rather than fear and avoidance. Therapy can provide additional support, offering a safe environment to explore the roots of your self-doubt and develop strategies for self-compassion. A therapist can guide you in identifying and dismantling the beliefs that fuel your inner critic, helping you build a foundation of resilience and self-worth.

Incorporating these strategies into your life takes time and patience, but each step brings you closer to living authentically, free from the shackles of self-doubt. The best and most effective way to silence the inner critic is to recognize its voice inside your head and choose not to let it define you. This is a choice you will make over and over again; keep making it. Every time you hear the inner critic in your mind, consider it a choice point; do you want to feed the inner critic, or do you want to choose to refute it? As you cultivate self-compassion and challenge negative thoughts, you'll find that your true potential is far greater than the critic ever allowed you to believe.

Struggles with Boundaries

Growing up with a narcissistic mother often means living in a world where your boundaries are invisible. This invisibility stems from a history where your personal space, both emotional and physical, was frequently disregarded. Imagine a childhood where your bedroom door was never truly yours to close, decisions about your life were made without your input, and your feelings were often dismissed as trivial. Your mother's needs and desires always took precedence, leaving little room for you to assert your own. Over time, this pattern becomes internalized. You learn that your boundaries are not worth defending, a mindset that follows you into adulthood, coloring your interactions with others.

The impact of these boundary issues is pervasive, often manifesting in both personal and professional spheres. In your personal life, you might find yourself overcommitting, agreeing to every request out of fear of displeasing others. This relentless cycle of saying yes leads to burnout as you stretch yourself thin trying to meet everyone's expectations. You might struggle to say no, feeling an overwhelming obligation to attend social events you have no interest in simply to avoid conflict or disappointment. These situations can leave you feeling drained and resentful, caught in a loop of obligations that offer little personal satisfaction. Professionally, the inability to set boundaries can result in taking on more work than you can handle, often without the recognition you deserve. This can lead to exhaustion, as you expend energy trying to prove your worth while neglecting your own well-being.

Consider the scenario where you feel obliged to attend a colleague's party despite having other plans for self-care. The pressure to conform to social norms overrides your personal needs, reflecting a pattern established in childhood. You find yourself in a room full of people, physically present yet emotionally absent, longing for the quiet comfort of your own space. This internal conflict is a direct consequence of blurred boundaries, where others' expectations overshadow your own desires. Such scenarios are commonplace, highlighting the struggle to prioritize your needs without guilt or anxiety.

Establishing healthy boundaries is a crucial step in reclaiming your autonomy. Start by role-playing boundary-setting conversations with a trusted friend or therapist. This exercise allows you to practice articulating your needs in a safe environment, building confidence for real-world interactions. Develop a personal boundary checklist outlining specific areas where you need to assert your limits. This checklist serves as a tangible reminder of your priorities, helping you stay focused when faced with demands that test your resolve. It might include simple affirmations like, "I deserve time for myself," or "It's okay to decline invitations." These affirmations reinforce your right to say no without guilt, empowering you to protect your time and energy.

Another effective strategy is to set aside time each week for self-reflection. Use this time to evaluate your commitments and assess whether they align with your values and needs. This reflection helps you identify patterns of overcommitment and provides insight into areas where boundaries need strengthening. Mindfulness practices, such as meditation or journaling, can aid in this self-reflection, offering clarity and focus. As you become more attuned to your needs, you'll find it easier to recognize when boundaries are being tested. This awareness is the first step towards asserting your right to set limits that honor your well-being.

Remember, establishing boundaries is not a one-time event but an ongoing process. It requires patience and persistence, as well as a willingness to prioritize your needs and well-being. As you practice setting and maintaining boundaries, you'll find that your relationships and self-esteem begin to flourish. You are worthy of respect and deserve to have your boundaries honored, both by others and by yourself.

Fear of Rejection and Abandonment

Growing up under the watchful eye of a narcissistic mother often means learning that love is not a given but something to be earned. This conditional love, where affection is contingent on meeting her expectations, breeds a profound fear of rejection and abandonment. As a child, you may have internalized the belief that your worth is tied to your ability to please, perform, or conform to her ideals. The anxiety of falling short of these expectations creates a looming fear of losing her approval and, by extension, her love. This fear doesn't just fade with time; it becomes a shadow that follows you into adulthood, silently influencing your interactions and relationships.

In your adult relationships, these fears can manifest as clinginess and neediness, driven by the underlying dread of being left behind. You might find yourself holding onto partners too tightly, afraid that any distance or disagreement could lead to abandonment. This anxiety can lead to behaviors that are counterproductive to healthy relationships. You might avoid conflict at all costs, believing that harmony is the only way to keep someone close. Instead of addressing issues directly, you suppress your feelings, fearing that expressing dissatisfaction might push your partner away. This avoidance can create a superficial peace while underlying problems remain unresolved, simmering beneath the surface.

The fear of rejection also pushes you to overcompensate in relationships, going above and beyond to gain approval. You may take on more than your fair share of responsibilities, always striving to prove your worth and indispensability. This drive to please can lead to exhaustion and resentment as you sacrifice your needs and desires in pursuit of validation. The irony is that in trying to hold onto relationships, these behaviors can strain them, creating the very outcome you fear most. The constant effort to be perfect and indispensable can be overwhelming for both you and your partner, leading to tension and dissatisfaction.

To address and alleviate these fears, consider exploring therapeutic approaches like attachment-based therapy. This form of therapy focuses on understanding how your early experiences with caregivers shape your current attachment styles. By examining these patterns, you can begin to reframe your understanding of relationships and develop healthier ways of connecting. This therapy can provide insights into the roots of your fears, helping you recognize that they stem from past experiences rather than present realities. Through this awareness, you can work towards building secure attachments where love and acceptance are not contingent on performance or perfection.

Engaging in self-reflection exercises can also be beneficial. Take time to identify the specific triggers that evoke your fear of rejection and abandonment. This might involve journaling about past experiences or exploring scenarios that heighten your anxiety. By pinpointing these triggers, you gain clarity about the situations or interactions that challenge your sense of security. Once identified, you can develop strategies to manage these triggers, whether through mindfulness techniques, open communication, or boundary-setting. This self-awareness empowers you to respond consciously, rather than reactively, to situations that test your fears.

Remember, overcoming these fears is not about erasing them entirely, but about learning to live with them and being understanding and compassionate. As you work through these challenges, seek support from trusted friends, therapists, or support groups who can provide perspective and encouragement. Surround yourself with relationships that reinforce your inherent worth, where love is given freely and unconditionally. As you practice these strategies, you may find that the fears of rejection and abandonment hold less power over you, allowing you to build genuine, fulfilling, and resilient connections.

The Quest for External Validation

Growing up with a narcissistic mother often means learning to measure self-worth through the eyes of others. This conditioning begins early, with praise and affection doled out as rewards for meeting her expectations. Compliance is seen as an achievement, the ticket to her approval, and anything less is met with disinterest or disdain. These interactions teach you to seek validation externally, as your own sense of worth becomes tangled with others' perceptions. The desire to please and be noticed by others becomes an intrinsic part of your identity, shaping how you see yourself and your accomplishments.

The consequences of this reliance on external validation are profound. When your self-worth hinges on external approval, personal achievements can feel hollow. You might struggle to appreciate your successes, always questioning whether they truly measure up. This mindset affects decision-making, as choices become less about personal fulfillment and more about how they'll be perceived by others. You might find yourself trapped in a cycle of seeking accolades, whether in the workplace or social circles, constantly chasing a sense of worthiness that remains elusive. This external focus can detract from genuine satisfaction, leaving you feeling unfulfilled despite outward success.

In various areas of life, the pursuit of validation is evident. In the workplace, you might tirelessly seek praise from superiors, viewing it as proof of competence. Promotions and accolades become benchmarks of your value, each one a temporary balm for deeper insecurities. On social media, the need for approval can manifest in a hunger for likes and comments, each interaction a fleeting affirmation of your significance. This craving for validation extends into personal relationships, where you might prioritize others' opinions over your own, bending to fit their expectations. This external focus can leave you disconnected from your true self as you mold your identity to match what you believe others desire.

Cultivating self-validation requires intentional effort and a shift in focus from external to internal sources of worth. One effective strategy is journaling personal achievements, a practice that allows you to celebrate your successes without external input. By documenting your accomplishments, both big and small, you create a tangible record of your growth, reinforcing your capabilities and worthiness. This practice encourages reflection and gratitude, helping you recognize your progress over time. Another effective exercise is practicing self-affirmation rituals. Begin each day with affirmations emphasizing your inherent value, independent of external approval. These affirmations can serve as powerful reminders that your worth is intrinsic, not contingent on others' recognition.

These practices help build a foundation of self-worth resilient to external fluctuations. They empower you to define success on your own terms, fostering a sense of fulfillment that is rooted in authenticity. As you shift your focus inward, you'll find that the need for external validation diminishes, replaced by a growing confidence in your abilities and choices. This internal validation creates a stable core from which you can navigate life's challenges with assurance and self-assuredness.

As you move through these concepts, it's important to acknowledge the impact of your past while embracing the potential for change. The patterns established in childhood do not have to dictate your future. With conscious effort and self-compassion, you can redefine your sense of worth, guided by an internal compass that honors your true self. In the next chapter, we will explore how to navigate ongoing relationships with narcissistic individuals, offering strategies to maintain your newfound sense of self within challenging dynamics.

Chapter 4
Breaking Free: Establishing Boundaries

You stand at the edge of a bustling family gathering, observing the familiar dynamics that have played out countless times before. Amid the laughter and chatter, your mother's voice carries, directing the flow of conversation with subtle precision. Her words, though seemingly benign, often leave you feeling small and uncertain. In these moments, the concept of boundaries becomes both a deep wish and a daunting challenge. It's a realization that the life you've lived has often blurred the lines between where you end and where others begin. Yet, the promise of boundaries is profound—offering the potential for clarity and peace in your relationships and within yourself.

Understanding boundaries begins with defining what they are and recognizing their vital role in maintaining mental health and well-being. Boundaries are the invisible lines that delineate where your needs and emotions separate from those of others. They serve as a form of self-care, safeguarding your personal time and energy from being depleted by external demands. Establishing boundaries is an act of self-preservation, a way to honor your limits and ensure that your well-being remains a priority. By setting these parameters, you create a space where your needs are acknowledged and respected, reducing the risk of burnout and emotional exhaustion. This self-care is not a luxury but a necessity, allowing you to engage with the world from a place of strength and balance.

In relationships, boundaries play a crucial role in fostering balanced and respectful interactions. They act as a framework within which healthy connections can thrive, preventing the overstepping of personal limits that often lead to resentment and conflict. Without boundaries, relationships can become one-sided, where one person's needs consistently overshadow the other's. This imbalance breeds frustration and emotional fatigue as you find yourself giving more than you receive. Boundaries serve as a protective barrier, ensuring that your interactions are based on mutual respect and understanding. They enable you to communicate your needs clearly and assertively, fostering a dynamic where both parties can flourish. In this context, boundaries are bridges, not barriers, facilitating deeper connections rooted in respect and empathy.

Empowerment is an inherent benefit of establishing boundaries. By defining your limits, you enhance your self-respect and build confidence in your personal choices. Boundaries empower you to take control of your life, making decisions that align with your values and priorities. This autonomy is liberating, as it allows you to live authentically, guided by your inner compass rather than external pressures. The act of setting boundaries is a declaration of your worth, affirming that your needs and emotions are valid and deserving of consideration. As you assert your boundaries, you reinforce your sense of self, cultivating a confidence that permeates all areas of your life. This empowerment is transformative, enabling you to navigate relationships and challenges with grace and assurance.

However, the absence of boundaries can have significant consequences. When boundaries are weak or nonexistent, personal limits are often overstepped, leading to feelings of frustration and resentment. You may find yourself overwhelmed by others' demands, sacrificing your needs to accommodate theirs. This pattern can create a cycle of self-neglect, where your well-being is consistently compromised. Over time, this dynamic creates resentment, as unspoken expectations and unmet needs strain your relationships. The lack of boundaries leaves you vulnerable to manipulation and control as others take advantage of your willingness to accommodate. Recognizing these consequences is the first step towards change, highlighting the importance of establishing boundaries that honor your needs and protect your well-being.

Boundary Mapping

Take a moment to reflect on your current boundaries in different areas of your life. Create a "boundary map" by dividing a sheet of paper into sections labeled work, family, friends, and personal time. Write down specific boundaries you would like to establish or strengthen each section. Consider what makes you feel respected and valued in each context. Use this map as a guide to initiate conversations about boundaries, ensuring they align with your values and priorities. This exercise serves as a visual reminder of your commitment to self-care and empowerment, reinforcing the importance of boundaries in fostering and supporting a balanced and fulfilling life.

Scripts for Difficult Conversations

Starting a conversation about boundaries can feel daunting, especially when you've spent years accommodating others at the expense of your own needs. Yet, the power of a well-structured boundary-setting conversation can transform relationships and improve your mental well-being. Begin by using "I" statements to express your needs clearly and personally. For example, instead of saying, "You always interrupt me," try, "I feel overwhelmed when I'm interrupted and need some time to finish speaking." This approach centers the dialogue on your feelings rather than assigning blame, making it easier for the other person to understand your perspective without becoming defensive.

Choosing the right time and setting for the conversation is crucial. Avoid discussing boundaries in the heat of the moment, when emotions might be running high. Instead, select a calm environment where both parties have the time and space to engage thoughtfully. Perhaps it's over a quiet coffee, away from the distractions of daily life, allowing both of you to focus on the conversation at hand. Timing also involves considering the other person's readiness to hear what you have to say. Ensure both of you are receptive, increasing the likelihood of a productive dialogue.

Here's a sample script for addressing intrusive behavior to aid in this process: "I appreciate your concern, but I feel uncomfortable when my decisions are questioned in front of others. I'd like us to discuss these matters in private." This script is simple yet effective, clearly stating your discomfort and proposing a solution. It's important to adapt these templates to fit your personal style and the specifics of your relationships. Customizing your language ensures authenticity, making it more likely that your message will be received as intended.

Despite your best efforts, you might encounter resistance or pushback when setting boundaries. Staying calm and assertive is key when facing such challenges. Remind yourself that maintaining your boundaries is a form of self-respect, and it's okay to stand firm. If necessary, repeat your boundary calmly, emphasizing its importance to you. For instance, if a family member continues to press an issue you've asked them to avoid, you might say, "I've mentioned before that I'm not comfortable discussing this. Let's focus on something else." Consistent repetition reinforces your stance, signaling that your boundaries are non-negotiable.

Clarity and consistency in your communication are paramount. Mixed messages can undermine your efforts, leading to confusion and frustration. Ensure that your words align with your actions; if you set a boundary, be prepared to enforce it. Consistency builds trust, showing others that you mean what you say. Regular reinforcement of boundaries is also essential, especially in relationships with deeply entrenched behavior patterns. By consistently upholding your boundaries, you create an environment where respect becomes the norm, not the exception.

Crafting Your Own Script

Take a moment to think about a boundary you wish to set. Write down a brief script using "I" statements to articulate your needs. Reflect on the timing and setting that would best support this conversation. Consider potential pushback and how you might respond assertively. This exercise will help solidify your intentions and prepare you for the actual discussion, empowering you to communicate with confidence and clarity.

The Grey Rock Method

In the tumultuous interactions with a narcissistic mother, the Grey Rock Method emerges as a strategic tool to navigate these encounters with minimal emotional fallout. This technique, aptly named for its uninspiring appearance, involves becoming as unremarkable as a grey rock, devoid of emotional engagement and devoid of drama. The primary goal of using this method is to reduce the emotional intensity of interactions, thereby minimizing the drama and conflict that often accompany relationships with narcissistic individuals. By adopting this approach, you aim to make yourself less appealing as a target for emotional manipulation, ultimately encouraging the narcissistic person to lose interest in provoking you.

The Grey Rock Method is extremely beneficial in high-conflict interactions where emotions run high and rational discussions become impossible. You might find it helpful during family gatherings or when unexpected confrontations arise. To use this method effectively, focus on giving minimal factual and bland responses. Avoiding emotional reactions is key; by not providing feedback that can be used against you, you maintain control over the interaction. Suppose your mother criticizes your choices or provokes you during a conversation. Instead of engaging or defending yourself, you might simply respond with a neutral, "I see," or "That's interesting," without offering further explanation or defense. This lack of engagement discourages any escalation, as the narcissistic person finds no emotional fuel to feed off.

Day-to-day scenarios provide ample opportunities to practice grey rock communication. Imagine your mother calls to discuss a family event, subtly pressuring you to attend despite your prior commitments. Instead of diving into an explanation or making excuses, you might reply with, "I'll check my schedule," and leave it at that. Your response remains polite yet devoid of the emotional hooks that might lead to further pressure or guilt-tripping. Similarly, if faced with backhanded compliments or veiled critiques, a simple "Thank you for your input" can suffice, effectively closing the door on any potential conflict without engaging in it.

However, the Grey Rock Method is not without its challenges and limitations. It's important to recognize when this approach may not be sufficient, particularly when more direct action is necessary. If the narcissistic behavior escalates or becomes harmful, relying solely on grey rocking might not be adequate. In such cases, alternative strategies like seeking professional guidance or exploring more assertive boundary-setting techniques may be necessary. Additionally, using the Grey Rock Method over extended periods can be mentally exhausting, as it requires constant vigilance and emotional restraint. It's crucial to monitor your mental well-being and ensure you have the support and self-care practices in place to prevent burnout.

Another limitation is that some individuals with narcissistic tendencies may react unpredictably to the method. While some might lose interest, others may intensify their efforts to provoke a reaction. They might employ tactics such as love bombing, suddenly showering you with affection, or attempting to hoover you back into their sphere of influence. Be prepared for these possibilities and have a plan for maintaining your boundaries and emotional distance. Remember, the goal of grey rocking is not to change the other person but to protect yourself by reducing the emotional impact of their behavior. Recognizing when to use this technique and when to seek additional strategies is key to maintaining your stability and well-being in challenging interactions.

Saying No Without Guilt

Growing up, you may have learned that saying "no" was akin to disappointment, a mark of selfishness rather than self-care. This belief, often rooted in familial conditioning, can create an enduring fear of letting others down. In a household led by a narcissistic mother, your needs might have been secondary, and acquiescence was expected, molding your perception of self-worth to align with others' approval. This conditioning can lead to guilt when declining requests, as if prioritizing your well-being somehow diminishes your value. The psychological barriers to saying "no" often stem from a desire to maintain harmony and avoid conflict, leaving you trapped in a cycle of compliance that sacrifices personal needs for others' satisfaction. Over time, this fear of disappointing others can erode your confidence in setting limits, making it challenging to assert your boundaries without feeling guilty or selfish.

To confidently say "no," it's crucial to practice assertive language that communicates your needs clearly and respectfully. Begin by prioritizing your personal needs, acknowledging that they are as valid as anyone else's. This shift in perspective empowers you to view saying "no" as an act of self-respect rather than rejection. Consider using phrases that affirm your stance while maintaining politeness. For instance, when declining an invitation you're not interested in, a simple "I appreciate the offer, but I need to focus on other commitments right now" can communicate your decision firmly yet kindly. Practicing such responses helps build confidence, reducing the guilt associated with asserting your limits. It's also important to recognize that your time and energy are finite resources deserving of protection and mindful allocation.

Respectful refusal can also involve offering alternative solutions, which can soften the impact of a "no" while maintaining your boundaries. If a colleague asks for your help on a project, yet your schedule is already full, you might reply, "I can't assist this time, but I'd be happy to review your progress later." This approach both preserves your boundaries and supports collaboration without overextending yourself. Setting clear expectations in such scenarios reinforces your autonomy, ensuring that others understand your limits without ambiguity. This clarity is key to maintaining respectful relationships where your needs are honored alongside others.

Learning to say "no" brings significant benefits that extend beyond immediate interactions. It grants you more time for personal interests, allowing you to engage in activities that nourish your spirit and foster growth. This newfound freedom enables you to explore passions and hobbies that may have been sidelined due to constant obligations. By prioritizing your needs, you strengthen your personal autonomy, empowering yourself to make decisions that align with your values and desires. This empowerment leads to a reduction in stress as the pressure to please others diminishes, leaving you with the energy and focus to pursue meaningful endeavors. Embracing the ability to say "no" without guilt transforms your approach to relationships, fostering dynamics where mutual respect and understanding thrive.

As you integrate these strategies, consider the positive ripple effect on your overall well-being. By confidently asserting your boundaries, you cultivate a sense of agency that enriches every aspect of your life. This confidence enhances your relationships and reinforces your self-worth, affirming that you are deserving of respect and consideration. The practice of saying "no" becomes a testament to your growth as you navigate interactions with authenticity and self-assurance. Recognizing the power in refusal allows you to redefine your narrative, embracing a life where your needs are prioritized and your voice is heard.

Maintaining Boundaries Over Time

As you learn to manage the complexities of relationships, maintaining boundaries becomes an ongoing process, not a one-time event. Life is dynamic, and relationships evolve, so boundaries must adapt to these changes. What worked in one phase of your life might need adjustment as circumstances shift. This is why reinforcing boundaries regularly is crucial. It ensures that the lines you've drawn continue to serve your needs and protect your well-being. This continuous process of evaluation allows you to remain in control, adapting to new dynamics without losing sight of your priorities.

To ensure that your boundaries remain respected, it is helpful to reassess them periodically. Take time to reflect on your current limits and consider whether they still align with your values and circumstances. This practice of regular reassessment not only keeps your boundaries relevant but also strengthens your commitment to upholding them. As you identify areas that require adjustment, communicate any changes promptly. Clear communication prevents misunderstandings and reinforces your expectations. By articulating these adjustments, you reaffirm the importance of your boundaries, signaling to others that your needs are a priority.

When boundaries are ignored, it's very important to address violations directly. Confronting these situations can be uncomfortable, but it's necessary to prevent further transgressions. Approach the conversation with a calm and assertive demeanor, focusing on the specific behavior that crossed the line. By addressing the issue directly, you demonstrate that your boundaries are non-negotiable. If necessary, reassert the boundary to emphasize its significance. This might involve reiterating your expectations and clarifying any consequences for future violations. Consistent enforcement reinforces your boundaries, ensuring they are respected and upheld.

Self-reflection plays a vital role in maintaining effective boundaries. Periodically evaluate your interactions and identify areas where your boundaries may need strengthening. This reflection helps you recognize patterns of behavior that challenge your limits, allowing you to adapt accordingly. As life changes, so too might your needs and expectations. Adapting your boundaries to reflect these changes ensures they remain relevant and effective. This adaptability is a sign of growth, allowing you to handle life's challenges while maintaining your well-being. By embracing self-reflection and adjustment, you create a framework for boundaries that support your evolving journey.

In maintaining boundaries, you're protecting your well-being and establishing relationships built on respect and understanding. Your commitment to reinforcing these boundaries sends a powerful message about your worth and priorities. Each step you take in upholding your limits strengthens your autonomy and confidence. This empowerment extends beyond individual interactions, shaping how you engage with the world. As you refine your boundaries, you cultivate a life that honors your needs and aspirations. This chapter has explored the continuous nature of boundary maintenance, highlighting its role in creating healthy relationships. In the next chapter, we'll get into healing the emotional wounds left by childhood experiences, paving the way for a future defined by resilience and self-discovery.

Chapter 5
Healing Emotional Wounds

You find yourself standing in front of the mirror, scrutinizing every detail. The face staring back at you is familiar, yet any trace of self-assurance seems elusive. Each fleeting thought critiques another perceived flaw, echoing sentiments you've internalized since childhood. This constant self-evaluation feels exhausting, and in these moments, the concept of self-validation seems distant. Yet, it is precisely this skill that holds the key to breaking the cycle of self-doubt entrenched by a narcissistic mother. Self-validation is a powerful tool that supports self-esteem and autonomy, allowing you to recognize your inherent value without relying on external approval.

At its core, self-validation involves acknowledging your experiences and emotions as legitimate, independent of others' perceptions. This practice builds self-esteem by reinforcing that your thoughts and feelings matter. By recognizing personal achievements, you celebrate victories that might otherwise go unnoticed, nurturing a sense of accomplishment. This affirmation of your worth is vital for developing autonomy, empowering you to trust your judgments and decisions. As you learn to validate your worth, you begin to dismantle the belief that approval must come from others, creating a foundation for genuine self-confidence.

To cultivate self-validation, daily exercises can be transformative. Start with affirmations each morning, speaking positive truths about yourself into the day. These statements, such as "I am capable" or "My feelings are valid," serve as anchors, grounding you in self-worth. Positive self-talk routines offer reinforcement throughout the day, countering negative thoughts with affirming responses. When doubt creeps in, remind yourself of past successes, reinforcing your ability to overcome challenges. These practices, though simple, can reshape your mindset over time, fostering resilience and self-acceptance.

Self-compassion plays a crucial role in self-validation, acting as a balm for past wounds. By practicing forgiveness for past mistakes, you release the grip of guilt and regret, allowing space for healing. Embracing imperfections is equally important, as it acknowledges that flaws are part of the human experience, not indicators of failure. This acceptance allows a gentler internal dialogue, where self-criticism gives way to understanding and growth. As you nurture self-compassion, you create an environment where validation flourishes, grounded in the belief that you deserve kindness and respect.

Consider the journey of Sarah, who struggled with self-esteem after years of criticism. She began incorporating self-affirmation techniques into her routine, initially skeptical of their impact. Yet, over time, these affirmations transformed her self-perception. By acknowledging her achievements and practicing self-compassion, she began to see herself through a lens of empathy rather than judgment. This shift allowed Sarah to embrace her worth and strengths, fostering a newfound confidence that permeated her interactions and decisions.

Self-Validation Exercise: Daily Affirmation Journal

Create a daily affirmation journal to track your journey in self-validation. Each morning, write down three affirmations that resonate with you. Reflect on an achievement, big or small, and note how it made you feel. In the evening, review your entries, acknowledging any progress or challenges. This exercise takes very little time yet can have a significant impact. It encourages active participation in your growth, providing tangible evidence of your evolving self-perception. As you cultivate this practice, notice how your relationship with yourself transforms, paving the way for healing and empowerment.

As you engage with these exercises, remember that self-validation is an ongoing process that requires patience and consistency. Each step reinforces your worth and autonomy, empowering you to navigate life with confidence and authenticity.

Rebuilding Self-Trust

Self-trust is a vital foundation that, when strong, builds resilience and confidence to help you face every challenge. Self-trust is the unwavering belief in your ability to make sound decisions, even when doubt whispers otherwise. For daughters of narcissistic mothers, this trust is often elusive, undermined by years of criticism and control. You may find yourself questioning your instincts, second-guessing choices, or fearing mistakes. Yet, reclaiming self-trust is crucial. It serves as a foundation that supports personal growth, guiding you through uncertainty with assurance and clarity. Trusting your judgment empowers you to navigate life's complexities, knowing that your inner compass is reliable and true.

To rebuild and enhance self-trust, consider engaging in decision-making exercises. Start with small choices, such as a meal or a weekend activity. Embrace these decisions without seeking validation from others, reinforcing your ability to trust your judgment. Gradually, tackle more significant decisions, reflecting on the outcomes to learn and grow. Intuition-strengthening activities are also beneficial. Practice listening to your gut feelings in everyday situations, acknowledging them without immediate action. This practice fosters a connection with your inner voice, enhancing your confidence in its guidance. As you engage with these exercises, you'll find that your trust in yourself deepens, creating a sense of empowerment that permeates all aspects of life.

The impact of self-trust on personal growth is profound. As you regain trust in yourself, confidence naturally follows. You become more decisive, approaching life choices with assurance rather than hesitation. This confidence spills into your interactions, allowing you to communicate your needs and boundaries with clarity and conviction. Self-trust also promotes emotional growth as you learn to maneuver through challenges with resilience and adaptability. You become more attuned to your emotions, recognizing them as valuable guides rather than obstacles. This emotional intelligence enhances your relationships as you engage with others from a place of strength and self-assurance.

Consider the story of Emma, who, after years of self-doubt, began a journey to rebuild her self-trust. She started with small decisions, such as choosing her outfits without seeking approval. Over time, she tackled larger choices, like pursuing a new career path. Through each decision, Emma learned to trust her instincts, embracing mistakes as opportunities for growth. Her newfound confidence transformed her life, enabling her to set boundaries and pursue her passions without fear of judgment. Emma's experience illustrates the transformative power of self-trust, showcasing how it can propel you towards a more authentic and fulfilling life.

Intuition Journal

Create an intuition journal to document your experiences with trusting your instincts. Each day, record situations where you felt a gut reaction. Note whether you acted on it and what the outcome was. Over time, review your entries to identify patterns and insights, reinforcing your confidence in your intuitive abilities. This exercise strengthens self-trust and serves as a reminder of your capacity to tackle life's challenges with grace and assurance. As you engage with this practice, notice how your connection with your inner voice evolves, guiding you toward decisions that align with your values and desires.

Cognitive Restructuring for Emotional Clarity

In the whirlwind of emotions that often accompanies life as the daughter of a narcissistic mother, cognitive restructuring emerges as a pathway to clarity. This therapeutic tool offers a way to untangle the web of negative thought patterns that can distort your perception of reality. Cognitive restructuring is about recognizing and altering these patterns, enabling you to approach life with a clearer, more balanced mindset. At its heart lies the identification of cognitive distortions, those automatic thoughts that skew your understanding of yourself and the world. Whether it's catastrophizing a minor setback or seeing life in black and white, these distortions can intensify anxiety and undermine confidence. Reframing these thoughts is imperative, as it allows you to replace them with more realistic and positive alternatives, supporting resilience and emotional stability.

To truly harness the power of cognitive restructuring, engaging in practical exercises can be transformative. Start by keeping a thought diary to document negative thoughts as they arise. This practice encourages you to pause and reflect, shedding light on the patterns that often go unnoticed. Write down the situation, the thought, and the emotion it triggered. Over time, you'll begin to see recurring themes, providing insight into your cognitive biases. Complement this with the ABC model: identify the Activating event, pinpoint the Belief it triggered, and note the Consequence, or emotional response. By dissecting these components, you can challenge and modify the underlying beliefs, paving the way for healthier emotional reactions.

The benefits of cognitive restructuring are manifold. As you consistently apply these techniques, you may notice a reduction in anxiety and depression as the grip of negative thoughts loosens. Emotional clarity emerges, allowing you to navigate life's challenges with a sense of calm and confidence. This newfound resilience enhances your ability to face adversity, transforming once-daunting obstacles into opportunities for growth. By shifting your cognitive framework, you open the door to a more empowered existence where your thoughts support rather than sabotage your well-being.

Imagine a moment where you find yourself caught in the throes of self-criticism, convinced that a minor mistake at work signals impending failure. With cognitive restructuring, you pause, acknowledging the thought without judgment. You then challenge its validity, asking questions like, "Is this truly indicative of my capabilities?" or "Have I succeeded despite mistakes before?" This reframing allows you to transform a self-critical narrative into one of self-compassion and growth, shifting from "I can't do anything right" to "Mistakes are a part of learning, and I am capable of improvement." Such cognitive shifts are powerful, as they reshape your internal dialogue, fostering a more supportive and constructive mindset.

Thought Diary Template

Create a thought diary template to guide your cognitive restructuring practice. Divide a page into columns labeled: Situation, Thought, Emotion, and Alternative Thought. Use this template to track and analyze your cognitive patterns. Over time, review your entries to identify common distortions and practice reframing them. This exercise is wonderful for self-awareness and also empowers you to challenge and change negative thought patterns, paving the way for emotional clarity and resilience. As you engage with this practice, notice the transformation in your thought processes, as clarity replaces confusion, and empowerment takes the place of doubt.

Journaling for Emotional Release

Imagine opening a notebook, its blank pages inviting you to pour out the thoughts that have been swirling in your mind. Journaling can be a powerful in processing emotions and facilitating healing, especially for those who have grown up with narcissistic mothers. The act of writing serves as an emotional release, providing a safe space to express feelings that might otherwise remain bottled up. This cathartic process allows you to confront and explore emotions without judgment, leading to greater insight and understanding. By externalizing thoughts and emotions, journaling helps you untangle complex feelings, offering clarity and perspective that pave the way for healing.

One of the most effective journaling techniques is stream-of-consciousness writing. This method encourages you to write freely, without concern for grammar or structure, allowing thoughts to flow unencumbered. It's a way to access the subconscious and uncover hidden emotions or patterns that might be influencing your behavior. Another valuable approach is gratitude journaling, which shifts the focus from negative experiences to positive ones. By regularly noting things you're thankful for, no matter how small, you cultivate a mindset of appreciation that can counterbalance feelings of inadequacy or resentment. Gratitude journaling supports a more optimistic outlook, helping you recognize the positives in your life despite past challenges.

To guide your emotional exploration, consider prompts that get into significant experiences. For instance, you might write about a situation where you felt misunderstood. Reflect on what happened, how it made you feel, and why it affected you deeply. Such prompts encourage introspection, enabling you to explore underlying emotions and gain insight into your responses. This process enhances self-awareness and empowers you to articulate your feelings more clearly in future interactions. By regularly engaging with these prompts, you develop a deeper understanding of yourself and your emotional landscape, facilitating personal growth and healing.

The impact of journaling is evident in numerous testimonials. Take Laura, for example, who struggled with a persistent sense of confusion and disconnection after years of emotional neglect. Through journaling, she found a voice for her pain, articulating feelings she had long suppressed. As Laura wrote, she began to identify patterns and triggers, gaining clarity on her emotional responses. This newfound understanding allowed her to approach relationships with greater empathy and confidence. Journaling became a transformative practice, helping Laura to process her past and embrace a more authentic self. Her experience highlights how journaling can illuminate the path to healing, offering a tangible way to navigate the complexities of emotions and memories.

Journaling Prompts

Consider incorporating journaling prompts into your routine to deepen your emotional exploration. Here are a few to get started: "What is a memory that still feels unresolved?" "Describe a time when you felt truly seen." "Write about a fear that has been holding you back." Use these prompts as starting points, allowing your thoughts to unfold naturally. As you engage with these exercises, observe how your perspective shifts, and how the act of writing brings clarity to your emotions and experiences. This practice nurtures self-discovery and also serves as a powerful tool for healing, helping you to process and understand the layers of your emotional world.

In your journey with journaling, remember that there is no right or wrong way to engage with the practice. It's a personal tool meant to serve your unique needs, allowing you to explore and express in whatever way feels most authentic. Through the act of writing, you create a space where your emotions are acknowledged and respected, giving you a sense of empowerment and healing.

Visualization for Healing

Visualization is an incredibly effective tool for emotional healing, especially for an adult daughter of a narcissistic mother. Growing up in an environment where love and acceptance were often conditional, you may have internalized feelings of inadequacy, self-doubt, or an overbearing need for validation. Visualization helps you break free from these patterns by allowing you to reimagine your inner world. Through consistent practice, you can create a mental space where you feel safe, valued, and supported; something you may not have experienced in your formative years. This mental exercise can serve as a foundation for rebuilding your sense of self-worth and creating a life driven by your own values rather than the expectations of others.

One of the most significant benefits of visualization is its ability to soothe the nervous system and promote emotional regulation. When you visualize yourself in a serene environment, such as walking through a peaceful forest or sitting by the ocean, you activate your parasympathetic nervous system, which helps reduce stress and anxiety. For those who have endured chronic emotional stress from a narcissistic parent, this practice can be particularly grounding. It allows you to step away from the internalized chaos and criticism and cultivate a sense of inner peace and balance.

Additionally, visualization can be instrumental in setting and reinforcing boundaries. Many adult daughters of narcissistic mothers struggle with asserting their needs due to a history of being dismissed or punished for doing so. By visualizing scenarios where you confidently set boundaries, you can rehearse this skill in a low-pressure, safe environment. This mental rehearsal strengthens your ability to act decisively and calmly in real life situations. Over time, these visualizations empower you to prioritize your well-being and develop healthier interpersonal dynamics.

Mindfulness Practices for Healing

Mindfulness offers a path to healing that centers on the present moment, providing a refuge from the chaos of past and future worries. It invites you to engage fully with the now, reducing stress and anxiety by anchoring your awareness to what's immediate and tangible. This practice is especially beneficial for those who have endured the emotional turbulence of a narcissistic upbringing, where the past often casts long shadows over the present. By focusing on the here and now, mindfulness helps diminish the grip of distressing memories, allowing you to experience life with clarity and calm. It encourages a gentle observation of thoughts and feelings without judgment, fostering a state of acceptance and balance. This shift in focus can alleviate the habitual tension that arises from dwelling on past hurts or anticipating future challenges, offering relief and a sense of peace.

Incorporating mindfulness into your daily routine can be simple yet profoundly transformative. Mindful breathing techniques serve as an accessible entry point. Begin by taking a few deep breaths, drawing air into your lungs slowly and deeply. Pay attention to the sensation of the breath entering and leaving your body, noticing how it calms and centers you. If your mind begins to wander, gently bring your focus back to your breath. This practice calms the mind and establishes a connection with your body, grounding you in the present moment. Another effective exercise is the body scan meditation, which involves tuning into each part of your body in succession. Starting at your toes, gradually move your awareness upward, observing any tension or sensations without trying to change them. This meditative practice enhances your awareness of physical and emotional states, encouraging relaxation and emotional release.

The psychological benefits of mindfulness extend beyond stress reduction. As you cultivate mindfulness, you develop improved emotional regulation, which enhances your ability to respond to life's challenges with composure and resilience. By observing emotions without attachment, you learn to navigate them with greater ease, reducing their power to overwhelm. Mindfulness also fosters increased self-compassion, as it encourages you to treat yourself with the same kindness and understanding you would offer a friend. This compassionate perspective softens self-criticism, allowing you to embrace your imperfections and mistakes without harsh judgment. Over time, these practices can transform your relationship with yourself, nurturing a sense of inner peace and well-being.

Consider the story of Lisa, who struggled with severe anxiety following years of emotional neglect from her narcissistic mother. She turned to mindfulness meditation as a last resort, skeptical of its potential impact. Yet, as she committed to regular practice, Lisa noticed a gradual shift. Mindfulness allowed her to step back from her anxious thoughts, observing them without becoming entangled. This newfound perspective diminished their hold over her, reducing the frequency and intensity of her anxiety episodes. Lisa's journey illustrates how mindfulness can empower individuals to reclaim control over their emotional landscape, fostering resilience and clarity in the face of adversity. Her experience highlights the transformative power of mindfulness, showcasing its capacity to cultivate a more balanced and fulfilling life.

As this chapter concludes, you have explored various avenues for healing emotional wounds, from self-validation to mindfulness. Each practice offers a unique way to rebuild your relationship with yourself, fostering growth and resilience. In the next chapter, we will dive into reclaiming your identity, continuing the journey towards a life defined by authenticity and empowerment.

Chapter 6
Reclaiming Identity

The mirror doesn't lie, but sometimes, it fails to reflect the soul within. Standing before it, you might see a familiar face framed by expectations and past judgments. Yet beneath the surface, your true self waits patiently, ready to emerge. This chapter invites you to embark on a profound exploration of identity, a quest to discover who you are beyond the roles assigned by a narcissistic mother or societal norms. It is an opportunity to uncover the unique beauty and strength of your being, from your interests, values, and dreams, all waiting to be acknowledged and celebrated.

Understanding your true self begins with introspection, a journey into the heart of your desires and passions, free from external demands. Reflective journaling serves as a powerful tool in this process. As you put pen to paper, allow your thoughts to flow unrestrained, capturing your interests and aspirations without judgment. Let this practice be a sanctuary where your dreams can take shape, revealing patterns and passions that resonate deeply. Consider the hobbies and activities that light you up, those moments when time seems to slip away. These are the clues to your authentic self, guiding you toward a life that aligns with your innermost yearnings.

Yet, barriers rooted in lingering maternal influence and societal expectations often obscure the path to self-awareness. The pressure to conform to a mother's ideals or fit into societal molds can create a distorted sense of self. You may find yourself acting out roles defined by others, sacrificing your desires to meet their approval. This pressure can lead to a disconnect between who you are and who you think you should be, leaving you feeling fragmented and unsure. Recognizing these barriers is crucial for reclaiming your identity. Acknowledge the weight of these expectations, and give yourself permission to redefine who you are on your own terms.

Methods for gaining clarity on your personal identity can provide a roadmap for this transformative journey. Personality assessments, such as the Myers-Briggs Type Indicator or the Enneagram, offer insights into your natural tendencies and preferences. These tools can illuminate aspects of your personality, helping you understand how you interact with the world. Similarly, analyzing your strengths and weaknesses provides valuable information about your capabilities and areas for growth. This self-awareness empowers you to make informed decisions, guiding you toward a path that honors your unique attributes. As you gain clarity, you can begin to align your life with your authentic self, creating a foundation for fulfillment and happiness.

Consider the story of Maya, who spent years in a career chosen to satisfy her parents' expectations. Despite her success, she felt unfulfilled, her true passions buried beneath layers of obligation. Through introspection and self-discovery exercises, Maya unearthed a love for art that had been dormant since childhood. Embracing this passion, she pursued a path as an artist, breaking free from the constraints of familial pressure. Her journey illustrates the power of self-awareness in transforming one's life.

By aligning her career with her authentic self, Maya found joy and purpose, redefining success on her own terms.

Another compelling example is Jasmine, who grew up in a family with rigid expectations, leaving little room for individuality. She felt trapped in a cycle of pleasing others, her own desires overshadowed by obligation. Through self-discovery practices, Jasmine identified her core values, realizing her true calling lay in social work. Despite familial pressure to pursue a conventional career, Jasmine followed her heart, dedicating herself to a path that resonated with her values. Her decision to embrace her authentic self not only brought fulfillment but also inspired others to pursue their passions. Jasmine's story highlights the transformative impact of reclaiming one's identity, illustrating that self-discovery is a courageous and rewarding endeavor.

Your Ideal Self

Visualize your life free from external expectations. What passions would you pursue? What values guide your decisions? Create a vision board to capture these reflections, using images and words that resonate with your ideal self. This visual representation serves as motivation, guiding you toward a life free from the echos of your mother's narcissistic legacy and toward one that honors your true identity.

Differentiating Between Your Voice and Theirs

The echoes of maternal voices can linger long into adulthood, casting shadows over your self-perception and clouding your judgment. When a mother's critical words become the internal dialogue you hear daily, distinguishing between your own thoughts and the criticisms ingrained by years of parental influence can be challenging. These internalized messages often mirror her voice, replaying doubts and criticisms that undermine confidence and autonomy. You might find yourself questioning each decision, wondering if it's truly yours or simply an echo of what you've been told to believe. This critical inner dialogue can become so entrenched that making independent decisions feels daunting as if every choice must first pass through the filter of maternal approval. The result is a life lived in hesitation and doubt, where your authentic voice struggles to be heard above the noise of inherited judgments.

To reclaim your voice and separate it from these external influences, mindful meditation offers a path to awareness. This practice encourages you to sit quietly with your thoughts, observing them without judgment. As you meditate, notice which thoughts reflect your true desires and which are echoes of past criticisms. This awareness allows you to begin disentangling the two, creating space for your authentic voice to emerge. Another technique is to question the origin of your beliefs. When a critical thought arises, ask yourself if it aligns with your values or if it stems from someone else's expectations. Through consistent practice, these strategies help you identify and affirm your beliefs, making room for your voice to guide your decisions.

Rediscovering your voice is a powerful act of empowerment, one that builds confidence and clarity in decision-making. As you learn to trust your inner voice, you can pursue personal goals without fearing judgment or disapproval. This freedom is transformative, allowing you to define success on your own terms and embrace a life that reflects your true self. The process of reclaiming your voice promotes self-assurance, enabling you to articulate your needs and desires with conviction. It is an opportunity to step into your power to make choices that resonate with your soul rather than simply conforming to the expectations of others.

Consider the story of Emma, who spent years enduring her mother's criticism, believing that every decision had to meet her approval. Emma's critical inner dialogue echoed her mother's voice, leaving her paralyzed with indecision. It wasn't until she began practicing mindful meditation that Emma started recognizing her own thoughts. She realized that her passion for writing, once dismissed by her mother as impractical, was her true calling. Trusting her intuition, Emma pursued a career in writing, finding fulfillment and validation in her own voice. Her story illustrates the profound impact of distinguishing personal beliefs from imposed ones, highlighting the freedom that comes with embracing one's authentic self.

Embracing Authenticity

Authenticity is the heartbeat of personal growth. It's about living in alignment with your true values and beliefs, allowing you to build genuine relationships and find fulfillment. When you live authentically, you are not just existing but thriving. It means honoring your own principles, even when they don't always align with the expectations of others. Authenticity allows you to connect deeply with those around you, forming relationships that are sincere and meaningful. These connections are based on mutual respect and understanding rather than pretense or obligation. Living authentically brings joy and satisfaction, as your actions and decisions reflect your true self, leading to a more complete and balanced life.

However, embracing authenticity is not without its challenges. Societal and familial pressures often make this a daunting task. The fear of judgment or rejection looms large, as stepping outside the norm can lead to criticism or alienation. You might find yourself caught in a web of expectations where authenticity feels risky. The pressure to conform can be overwhelming, pushing you to wear masks that hide your true self. But these masks, though protective, can become stifling, preventing you from experiencing the freedom and happiness that come with living authentically. Understanding these pressures is the first step toward overcoming them. Recognizing the fear of judgment allows you to confront it, finding strength in vulnerability and courage in truth.

To cultivate authenticity, start by setting intentions that align with your personal values. Take time to reflect on what truly matters to you, and let those values guide your actions. Begin each day with a clear intention and a commitment to honor your principles in every decision you make. This practice helps you stay grounded, reminding you of your core beliefs even when faced with external pressures. Practicing honesty in interactions is another crucial step. Speak your truth with kindness and clarity, ensuring your communications reflect your genuine thoughts and feelings. This honesty encourages trust and respect, both for yourself and others, creating a foundation for authentic relationships.

Consider the story of Jasmine, who worked a job that didn't fulfill her. Jasmine's mother had made it clear she expected Jasmine to be in the financial industry and to be very successful. Driven by her mother's expectations and a desire for security, she stayed on Wall Street for years, feeling disconnected and unhappy. Becoming more and more depressed and suffering from overwhelming anxiety, she finally said enough is enough. Jasmine decided to leave the career she never enjoyed, risk her mother's alienation, and pursue her passion for sustainable energy, a path that resonated with her values. Despite knowing there would be cascading strife and emotional backlash (both subtle and overt) from her mother, Jasmine embraced her authentic self, followed her passions, and found joy and purpose in her work. Jasmine's decision to live authentically transformed her career and enriched her life and relationships, as she surrounded herself with like-minded individuals who shared her vision. Jasmine's journey illustrates the profound impact of aligning one's life with personal passions, highlighting the fulfillment that comes with authenticity.

Another inspiring example is Rachel, who lived much of her life to please her mother and avoid being emotionally abandoned by her mother. Rachel was always emotionally and mentally drained because she was constantly trying to adapt to fit the needs and desires of those around her. It wasn't until Rachel began practicing authenticity that her life changed. She started by expressing her needs and setting boundaries, prioritizing honesty in her interactions. It was hard for Rachel at first, but the more she trusted the process the better she began to feel. She noticed an increase in her energy and a new excitement for her life. As Rachel embraced her true self, her relationships deepened, evolving into connections built on mutual respect and understanding. Her authenticity encouraged those around her to do the same, creating a close friend group where everyone felt seen and valued. Rachel's story demonstrates that living authentically is not just a personal transformation but a catalyst for change in the world around you.

Cultivating Self-Acceptance

In the quiet moments of reflection, when the noise of the world fades, the importance of self-acceptance becomes clear. It's not just a buzzword or a fleeting trend but a cornerstone of mental health. Embracing who you are in all aspects of your personality can lead to a profound sense of well-being. Self-acceptance acts as a balm, soothing the anxieties that often stem from harsh self-criticism and doubt. As you begin to accept yourself, you may notice a reduction in the relentless anxiety that once shadowed your every move. This acceptance allows you to breathe easier, walk lighter, and face the world with a newfound confidence. Improved self-esteem naturally follows, as the internal voice that once tore you down becomes a gentle reminder of your worth.

Yet, this path to self-acceptance is not without its hurdles. Internalized criticism, often inherited from childhood, can be a formidable adversary. Growing up with a narcissistic mother might have ingrained a sense of perfectionism, where nothing you did was ever quite enough. These internal voices can echo throughout your life, making self-acceptance seem like an unattainable goal. You might find yourself trapped in a cycle of striving for perfection, believing that only through flawlessness can you be worthy of love and respect. This pursuit is exhausting, leaving little room for the compassion and kindness that self-acceptance requires. It's easy to get caught in this web of self-judgment, but recognizing its presence is the first step toward untangling yourself from its grip.

To nurture a relationship with yourself that is rooted in acceptance, daily self-compassion practices can be transformative. Start with simple affirmations that celebrate your strengths and acknowledge your imperfections. These words, spoken with intention, can gradually shift your inner dialogue from one of criticism to one of understanding. Gratitude exercises focused on personal attributes can also encourage and support self-acceptance. Each day, take a moment to reflect on qualities you appreciate in yourself, whether it's your resilience, creativity, or kindness. These reflections help you recognize the value within, independent of external validation. Over time, these practices create a foundation of self-acceptance, allowing you to embrace your true self without reservation.

Consider the story of Amy, who battled self-criticism for years. Therapy, alongside daily affirmations, became her lifeline. Through these practices, Amy learned to challenge the negative beliefs that had dominated her thoughts. She began to see herself through a lens of compassion, celebrating her achievements and forgiving her missteps. Amy's journey illustrates the power of self-acceptance in transforming one's life. As she embraced herself fully, her anxiety diminished, and her confidence soared. This narrative serves as a testament to the impact of self-acceptance, providing hope and inspiration for anyone on the path to embracing their authentic self.

Building a Life of Your Own

Creating a life that truly reflects your identity is an empowering and satisfying endeavor. It begins with setting personal goals that align with your values and priorities. These goals serve as motivation, guiding you toward a future that resonates with your authentic self. To start, take a moment to envision what a fulfilling life looks like for you. Is it rooted in creativity, community, or adventure? Once you have a vision, break it down into actionable steps. Establish short-term and long-term goals that will help you move closer to this ideal. These goals are not just aspirations; they are commitments to yourself and promises to live in a way that honors who you are. By focusing on what truly matters, you lay the foundation for a life that is both meaningful and uniquely yours.

However, building an independent life is not without its challenges. The fear of change can be daunting, a shadow that looms over every decision. It whispers that the unknown is filled with risks and uncertainties. Yet, it is often in these uncharted territories that growth occurs. Embrace this fear as a natural part of the process, a sign that you are stepping into new possibilities. External disapproval can also pose significant obstacles, particularly from family members who may have different expectations. Managing these expectations requires courage and resilience. It means standing firm in your choices, even when they diverge from the path others envisioned for you. Overcoming the fear of the unknown involves trusting your ability to navigate challenges and adapt to new circumstances. This trust is built through experience and reflection, reinforcing your capacity to thrive in unfamiliar situations.

To take control of your life, consider crafting a chart or a vision board. This visual tool serves as a tangible representation of your aspirations and dreams. Fill it with images and words that inspire you and speak to the life you wish to create. Place it somewhere visible as a daily reminder of your goals and the steps needed to achieve them. Alongside this, develop a personal action plan. Outline specific actions required to reach your goals, complete with timelines and milestones. This plan acts as an outline for your future, providing structure and accountability as you move forward. It's a blueprint for transformation, a strategic approach to building the life you desire.

Consider the story of Shannon, who relocated to a new city, seeking personal growth and new opportunities. Despite the initial challenges of starting over, Shannon embraced the change, using it as a catalyst for reinvention. She found a community that shared her values and passions, enriching her life with diverse experiences. Her journey illustrates the power of change in fostering growth and fulfillment. Similarly, think of Lily, who pursued an unconventional career path despite skepticism from those around her and clear disapproval from her mother. She followed her passion for culinary arts, leaving a stable job to open her own bakery. Her determination and creativity brought her success and inspired others to pursue their dreams. Lily's story highlights the importance of staying true to oneself, even in the face of doubt.

With these insights, you can begin to craft your own story, one where your identity is the guiding star. Each step you take toward building a life that reflects your true self is a testament to your strength and authenticity. The challenges you face are opportunities for growth, shaping you into the person you are meant to be. As you travel along this path, remember that you are not alone. Others have walked similar roads, and their stories serve as confirmation and inspiration. In building a life of your own, you reclaim your power and write your own narrative. The future is yours to create, filled with possibilities as vast as your dreams. With the foundation of your true self firmly in place, you are ready to explore the vast opportunities that lie ahead.

Chapter 7
Empowerment and Personal Growth

Standing at the crossroads of your life, you may feel the weight of your past pulling against the promise of your future. Picture yourself standing on a vast plain, the horizon stretching endlessly before you. Your path may not be immediately apparent, but it is yours to forge. Setting personal goals becomes your guide, leading you through the challenges of your journey toward empowerment and personal growth. Goals provide a sense of direction and structure, charting the course from where you are to where you wish to be. They transform dreams into actionable steps, infusing your life with purpose and motivation. Without clear goals, it's easy to drift aimlessly, carried by external influences and expectations. With them, you harness the power of intention, focusing your energy and resources towards meaningful progress.

Personal goals act as milestones, marking achievements along your path and reinforcing your sense of accomplishment. Whether it's advancing your career, nurturing relationships, or cultivating a new skill, each goal represents a commitment to your growth. They enhance focus, allowing you to prioritize what truly matters, and boost productivity by channeling your efforts towards specific, desired outcomes. This clarity helps you overcome distractions, maintaining your course even when challenges arise. Setting goals organizes your aspirations and empowers you to take ownership of your life, instilling a sense of agency and control that is especially significant for those who have felt controlled or overshadowed by a narcissistic mother.

A structured approach to goal-setting can enhance this process, making it more effective and rewarding. One such method is the SMART framework, which stands for Specific, Measurable, Achievable, Relevant, and Time-bound. By defining goals that are clear and attainable, you set yourself up for success. A specific goal eliminates ambiguity, providing a clear target.

The SMART framework is a practical and effective tool for addressing emotional challenges, including the fear of abandonment often carried by adult daughters of narcissistic mothers. This fear, deeply rooted in childhood experiences of emotional neglect or manipulation, can feel overwhelming, but breaking it into manageable steps using the SMART method can make the healing process more achievable and empowering.

Specific: Start by clearly defining the goal you want to achieve. Instead of setting a vague objective like "stop feeling afraid of abandonment," create a focused goal such as, "I will practice self-compassion by using daily affirmations and journaling about moments when I felt secure." A specific goal eliminates uncertainty and provides a clear path forward.

Measurable: Being able to track progress is essential for staying motivated. For instance, you might measure your growth by noting each day you reframed a negative thought about abandonment or completed a self-compassion exercise. Keeping a journal or checklist allows you to see tangible evidence of your efforts, reinforcing your sense of achievement and motivating you to continue.

Achievable: Healing from deep-seated fears is a journey that requires patience, so it's important to set realistic goals. Instead of expecting to fully eliminate the fear in a short period, commit to small, manageable steps, such as challenging one negative thought each day or practicing mindfulness for five minutes when feelings of abandonment arise. These smaller goals are more practical and less overwhelming, helping you build confidence gradually.

Relevant: Your goal should align with your broader aspirations and values. Overcoming your fear of abandonment involves reducing anxiety, creating healthier relationships, building self-worth, and freeing yourself from patterns instilled during childhood. Framing your goal as part of this larger picture makes it deeply meaningful and keeps you connected to your purpose.

Time-bound: Finally, establish a timeframe to guide your progress and create a sense of accountability. For example, you might set a goal like, "Over the next three months, I will complete one journaling session daily and one therapy exercise weekly to address my fear of abandonment." A clear timeline provides structure, while also allowing flexibility for personal growth.

By using the SMART framework, you can transform an overwhelming challenge into a series of clear, accomplishable steps. This process helps you work through your fear of abandonment and empowers you to take control of your emotional healing. Through consistent effort and a structured approach, you can build a stronger, more confident version of yourself, free from the shadows of your past.

Another aspect to consider is the many psychological benefits of goal-setting that extend beyond the tangible. Achieving goals boosts self-esteem, affirms your capabilities, and fosters a positive, self-reinforcing sense of pride. Each milestone reached serves as a reminder of your potential, reinforcing confidence in your abilities. This confidence fuels further motivation, creating a positive cycle of empowerment and achievement. The satisfaction derived from reaching a goal is not merely about the outcome; it's about the growth and persistence demonstrated along the way. This sense of accomplishment encourages continued effort, propelling you towards even greater heights.

Here are two accounts of women who used the SMART method to help move forward in their lives. Jessica set a goal to heal from the emotional wounds caused by her narcissistic mother. She identified specific areas for growth, such as building self-esteem and learning to set healthy boundaries. She pursued these goals by attending therapy, reading self-help books, and practicing self-compassion through journaling and affirmations. Over time, her dedication paid off; she began feeling more confident in her decisions, recognized her worth, and established healthier relationships. Her journey exemplifies how targeted personal development can lead to significant emotional and relational growth, even in the aftermath of a challenging upbringing.

Another example involves Lisa, who aimed to overcome her fear of abandonment, a fear rooted in her childhood experiences with a narcissistic mother. She began by setting small, manageable goals, such as identifying and challenging negative thoughts, practicing mindfulness to manage anxiety, and seeking support from trusted friends or support groups.

Gradually, she expanded her efforts to include visualization exercises and inner child healing practices. The changes she embraced transformed her emotional well-being, illustrating the profound impact of personal goals on healing and reclaiming one's life from the shadows of the past.

Goal-Setting Vision Board

Create a vision board to represent your personal goals visually. Gather images, quotes, and symbols that resonate with your aspirations. Arrange them on a board or digital platform to remind you daily of your objectives and motivations. This exercise encourages creativity and reflection, inspiring as you work towards your goals.

As you begin setting and achieving personal goals, remember that each step, no matter how small, brings you closer to a life of empowerment and fulfillment. Your goals are more than destinations; they are the pathways to discovering and embracing your true potential.

Developing Resilience

Resilience is the invisible armor that helps you withstand the challenges of life. It's about learning to navigate these challenges with strength and adaptability. Think of resilience as a mental toughness that allows you to bounce back from adversity, even when the odds seem stacked against you. It's the ability to face setbacks head-on and emerge whole and stronger. This quality is necessary for personal growth, as it empowers you to endure and learn from difficulties. In a world where unpredictability is the norm, resilience is your steadfast guide, ensuring that no matter how hard you fall, you always find a way to rise.

Building resilience involves adopting strategies that strengthen your mental and emotional core. One method is practicing adaptive thinking, which involves viewing challenges as opportunities for growth rather than insurmountable obstacles. This mindset shift encourages you to reframe negative experiences, focusing on the lessons they offer. Another key strategy is learning from past experiences. Reflect on previous challenges you've overcome and the tactics that helped you succeed. These reflections can bolster your confidence, reminding you of your capability to handle future adversities. Embracing these strategies requires patience and persistence, but over time, they cultivate a resilience that becomes second nature, guiding you through life's ebbs and flows with grace and determination.

Resilience is pivotal in overcoming obstacles, contributing significantly to personal empowerment and long-term success. When you maintain focus during difficult times, resilience acts as your anchor. It keeps you grounded, allowing you to handle unforeseen upsets without losing sight of your goals. This focus empowers you to tackle challenges with clarity and determination, preventing temporary setbacks from derailing your progress. Overcoming obstacles through resilience builds confidence and reinforces your belief in your own strength and potential. It's a powerful reminder that no challenge is insurmountable when you approach it with resolve and adaptability. This resilience fuels your journey, transforming challenges into stepping stones towards success.

Consider the story of Juanita, an adult daughter of a narcissistic mother who set a goal to build resilience and reclaim her sense of self. She began by identifying specific areas where she wanted to grow, such as strengthening her self-esteem and learning to set healthy boundaries. To support her healing journey, Juanita sought therapy, practiced daily affirmations, and started journaling to explore her emotions and patterns of behavior. Over time, her consistent efforts paid off, and she began to recognize her worth, feel more confident in her decisions, and establish relationships based on mutual respect and support. Juanita's story shows how intentional steps helped her build resilience and empowered her to move beyond the pain of her past.

Another example involves Susan, who focused on overcoming the emotional triggers and fears instilled by her narcissistic mother, such as the fear of abandonment and the need for constant validation. She set small, manageable goals, like pausing to reflect before reacting, practicing mindfulness to calm her thoughts, and reframing negative beliefs she had internalized as a child. Gradually, she incorporated visualization techniques and inner child healing practices, reminding herself daily that she deserves love and respect. These practices strengthened Susan's emotional resilience, allowing her to face challenges with greater calm and self-assurance. Her healing journey highlights the transformative power of resilience, showing how it enables adult daughters to break free from the cycle of pain and embrace a life of authenticity and strength.

These narratives demonstrate that resilience is about more than just survival; it's about thriving in the face of adversity. It's about transforming challenges into opportunities for personal growth and empowerment. As you cultivate resilience, you give yourself the tools to oversee life's challenges with strength and grace, ensuring that every setback becomes a stepping stone towards a brighter, more fulfilling future.

Embracing Self-Care

Self-care is not a luxury; it's a necessity. It forms the backbone of both mental and physical well-being, acting as the cornerstone upon which health is built. Your life is a delicate balance, where the demands of work, family, and personal obligations often tip the scales. Without self-care, burnout becomes an all-too-common reality. Regular self-care practices help maintain equilibrium, preventing exhaustion from constantly giving without replenishing. It's about nurturing yourself, allowing you to be present and engaged in all areas of life. By prioritizing self-care, you lay a solid foundation for health, one that supports you through life's challenges and demands.

Incorporating self-care into your routine can take many forms tailored to your preferences and needs. Physical activities, like yoga or walking, offer a dual benefit, engaging the body while calming the mind. These practices encourage mindfulness, grounding you in the present moment and reducing stress. Creative outlets such as painting or writing provide a different kind of release, allowing you to express emotions and thoughts that might otherwise remain unspoken. Creativity can be cathartic, offering a space for exploration and self-discovery. Whether through movement or expression, these activities encourage a connection with yourself, promoting peace and fulfillment that permeates other aspects of your life.

Yet, embracing self-care is not without its challenges. Time constraints often serve as a formidable barrier. The demands of daily life can seem relentless, leaving little room for personal care. It's easy to push self-care aside, viewing it as less urgent than other responsibilities. However, overcoming this obstacle requires a shift in mindset. Time management strategies become very important, helping you carve out moments for yourself amidst the chaos. Consider scheduling self-care like any other appointment, with the same commitment and respect. Prioritizing self-care over other demands is not selfish; it's a necessary act of self-preservation, ensuring you have the energy and resilience to meet life's challenges head-on.

Take, for instance, the story of Mia, an adult daughter of a narcissistic mother, who struggled with intense anxiety and a deep fear of abandonment rooted in her childhood experiences. Feeling trapped in cycles of self-doubt, Mia decided to dedicate time each day to mindfulness practices, such as journaling and guided meditation, focused on self-compassion and emotional healing. Gradually, she noticed a change; the constant weight of anxiety lifted and was replaced by moments of peace and self-assurance.

Mia's journey illustrates the profound impact of consistent self-care. These small, intentional practices helped her reduce stress and rebuild a sense of control over her emotions and life. Her transformation was more than managing her anxiety; it was about reclaiming her worth, strengthening her resilience, and creating a future where she could truly thrive, free from the shadows of her past.

Self-care is a commitment to yourself, a declaration of self-worth that reinforces your value beyond productivity or external validation. It's an ongoing process, adapting to your needs as they evolve. As you embrace self-care, you create a sanctuary within your life, a refuge that sustains you through the inevitable ups and downs. This commitment to nurturing yourself reverberates through your interactions, relationships, and pursuits, enhancing your capacity to give and receive equally. Self-care becomes the key to living a balanced, fulfilling life in a world that often demands more than it gives.

Building a Supportive Community

Having a supportive community is like finding a safe and steady foundation during life's challenging moments. It's a space where you can ground yourself, surrounded by people who understand and uplift you. This community offers more than companionship; it provides emotional support and the motivation for personal growth. Here, you can share experiences and gain advice from those who have faced similar challenges, uncovering insights that truly resonate. The encouragement you receive propels you forward, while the accountability helps you stay focused on your goals. In this environment, vulnerability becomes a shared strength, fostering connections that empower you to face challenges with confidence and renewed energy.

Finding and building such a community may seem daunting, but it becomes an attainable goal with thoughtful steps. A community can be friends you have known your whole family, family members, colleagues from work, members from your religious affiliation, and new friends you seek out. Start by identifying your interests or passions, then look for groups or clubs that align with them. Whether it's a book club, a hobby group, or an online forum, these spaces are likely areas for forming meaningful connections. Participating in local events or workshops is another excellent way to meet like-minded individuals. These gatherings provide opportunities to engage in activities you enjoy while expanding your social network. Be open and approachable, willing to share your story and listen to others. Genuine curiosity and empathy are key to building a rapport that can develop into lasting friendships.

A supportive community will give you camaraderie and play a pivotal role in your personal development. It becomes a dynamic environment where learning and growth occur organically. Within this network, you exchange knowledge and skills, broadening your horizons and enhancing your understanding. You will begin to feel like yourself, have fun, and feel good. The diverse perspectives you will most likely encounter will challenge your assumptions, encouraging you to think critically and creatively. In a community, growth is a collective endeavor, with each member contributing to and benefiting from the shared journey of self-discovery and improvement. You will become both the mentor and the mentee, and this will feel very satisfying and boost your self-confidence and self-esteem.

A great example of how becoming a member of a community changes a person's life is Lilah. Lilah had spent most of her life chasing perfection, a mindset deeply ingrained by her narcissistic mother's constant criticism and impossible standards. Every decision felt like a test, and every mistake was proof of her inadequacy. The pressure left her emotionally drained, with mounting anxiety and a growing sense of depression. She began to feel trapped in a cycle of self-doubt, unsure how to break free.

One day, a friend suggested she try volunteering at a local dog shelter, and while hesitant at first, Lilah decided to give it a try. From the moment she walked through the doors, the warm, wagging tails and unspoken gratitude of the dogs offered her something she hadn't felt in years: unconditional love. Caring for the dogs gave Lilah a sense of purpose and accomplishment that wasn't tied to being perfect; it was simply about being present and kind. The shelter became her sanctuary, a place where she could let go of the expectations that had weighed her down for so long.

In addition to the emotional connection she formed with the animals, Lilah found herself bonding with the other volunteers. These new friendships felt genuine and supportive, a sharp contrast to the conditional relationships she had grown up with. Lilah felt validated for the first time, not because of her achievements, but because of who she was. The simple acts of walking a dog or cleaning a kennel became meaningful milestones, giving her a sense of pride and positivity she hadn't experienced before.

Over time, Lilah noticed a profound shift in her mindset. Her anxiety began to ease, and she felt lighter and more confident in her decisions. Volunteering at the shelter helped her see her own value outside of perfectionism, reignited a sense of joy and fulfillment in her life, improved her emotional well-being, and reminded her that she was worthy of love, compassion, and connection, just as she was.

Lilah's story illustrates the transformative power of a supportive community. It is a space where individual strengths are magnified through collective support, leading to personal and professional growth. Surrounding yourself with people who inspire and challenge you creates a fertile ground for development, and the bonds you form become an integral part of your journey. As you build and nurture this community, remember that it is a reciprocal relationship. The support and encouragement you give are as important as what you receive, creating a cycle of mutual empowerment and growth. Through the connections you cultivate, you not only find strength but also contribute to the strength of others, creating growth, shared experiences and aspirations.

Celebrating Achievements

Celebrating your achievements is more than just a momentary joy; it's an affirmation of your abilities and efforts. Recognizing your accomplishments is important because it reinforces positive behaviors and motivates you to continue striving for excellence. Each celebration reminds you of your progress, supporting a sense of pride and self-worth that bolsters your self-esteem. It's about acknowledging the hard work and dedication you've invested. This recognition validates your efforts and inspires you to set new goals, fueling a cycle of continuous growth and development. Celebrations, both big and small, create a narrative of success that empowers you to push further, even when challenges arise.

Finding creative ways to celebrate your milestones adds depth to these moments, making them memorable. Hosting small gatherings or personal ceremonies allows you to share your triumphs with those who support you, creating a communal experience of joy and reflection. These events need not be grand; even a simple dinner with close friends can be profoundly rewarding. Or you can do something just for yourself, like treating yourself to a manicure and pedicure. Alternatively, writing about your progress and accomplishments provides a personal space to reflect on your growth and can be exceptionally cathartic. Writing allows you to capture the emotions and learnings from your experiences as a tangible reminder of your achievements. This can be immensely fulfilling, as it helps you articulate the significance of your milestones, reinforcing their value and impact on your life.

The psychological benefits of celebrating your successes extend beyond the moment of recognition. Celebrations enhance emotional well-being by creating happy memories you can draw upon during challenging times. They become anchors of joy and pride, reminding you of your capabilities and resilience. This positive reinforcement strengthens self-belief, creating a mindset that embraces and anticipates future successes. As you celebrate, you reinforce the idea that you deserve happiness and fulfillment, which can profoundly impact your confidence and outlook. Recognizing your achievements cultivates an internal narrative of success, empowering you to face future endeavors with assurance and optimism.

Janine is a great example of how healing celebrations can be. Janine decided to celebrate her progress in healing from the emotional wounds inflicted by her narcissistic mother by taking a meaningful trip. She chose to visit a serene mountain retreat that symbolized strength and renewal. During her time there, she reflected on how far she had come in reclaiming her sense of self-worth and breaking free from the criticism and manipulation of her past. The trip allowed her to embrace her achievements, gain new insights about her journey, and return home feeling empowered and reconnected to her inner strength.

Another example of the impact that honoring your progress and achievements can have is Felice. Felice decided to mark her emotional growth by organizing a small celebration of her creativity and resilience. Having rediscovered her love for painting, a passion her narcissistic mother had dismissed, she hosted an art exhibition in her home. She displayed pieces representing her journey of self-discovery, inviting close friends who supported her healing process. Sharing her work in such an intimate setting affirmed her talent and validated her decision to embrace her passions despite past discouragement. This act of personal recognition celebrated her progress and fueled her determination to continue exploring and expressing her authentic self.

These stories highlight the transformative power of celebration. By taking the time to acknowledge your achievements, you nurture a mindset of positivity and resilience, empowering yourself to embrace future challenges with confidence. Celebrating your successes builds a foundation of self-assurance and motivation that supports you as you continue your personal growth and empowerment. As you recognize and honor your achievements, you amass a collection of meaningful experiences that reflect your journey toward a fulfilling and empowered life.

Chapter 8
Managing Ongoing Relationships

A daughter sits quietly in her living room, phone in hand, staring at the text message from her mother. She feels the familiar mix of dread and obligation. Her mother is demanding a visit, but the daughter knows the emotional toll it will take. It's a dance they've done many times before, one that leaves her exhausted and questioning her worth. For many adult daughters of narcissistic mothers, maintaining a relationship becomes a delicate balancing act. You want to honor the bond but protect yourself from the psychological strain it often brings. It's a struggle to find a way to coexist without losing yourself in the process.

Strategies for Limited Contact

Limited contact emerges as a lifeline, offering a way to preserve the relationship without compromising your well-being. At its core, limited contact involves setting clear boundaries around interactions, allowing you to engage with your mother on your terms. This approach balances maintaining familial ties and safeguarding your emotional space. By defining specific times for communication and setting boundaries around personal topics, you retain control over when and how interactions occur. This structure creates a buffer, reducing the likelihood of being caught off guard by unexpected demands or emotional manipulation.

Implementing limited contact requires careful psychological preparation. It begins with cultivating mental readiness and emotional resilience, essential tools for encounters with a narcissistic mother. Anticipating emotional triggers allows you to identify situations that may provoke anxiety or distress. Recognizing these triggers in advance will enable you to approach interactions clearly, minimizing their impact. Practicing emotional detachment techniques further strengthens your resolve. This involves maintaining a degree of separation between your mother's reactions and your self-worth, ensuring her words and actions don't infiltrate your sense of identity.

Once mentally prepared, you can establish limited contact through practical steps. Start by creating a communication schedule and deciding in advance when you will communicate with your mother. This might involve setting a specific day and time for calls or visits, providing structure and predictability. Technology can be a valuable ally in managing interactions. Utilize features like call screening or text messaging to control the flow of communication, responding only when you're ready. These tools empower you to engage on your terms, reinforcing your boundaries and reducing the potential for emotional ambushes.

The following scenario demonstrates where limited contact proves beneficial. Jane is a daughter who balances family obligations with her personal needs through strategic communication. She sets aside Sunday afternoons for her mother's calls, a time that allows her to be present without infringing on her own responsibilities. By establishing this routine, Jane created a predictable framework that minimizes conflict and maintains a sense of autonomy. And Christine, another daughter of a narcissistic mother, made a successful limited contact arrangement where she decided to limit in-person visits with her mother to once a month. She then takes ownership of the visit by choosing a neutral location for these meetings, reducing the potential for emotional confrontation within the family home. This approach has given Christine a sense of control and clarity, allowing her to engage without feeling overwhelmed.

Crafting Your Limited Contact Plan

Reflect on your current relationship dynamics and consider how limited contact might benefit you. Identify specific boundaries you wish to establish, such as communication frequency or topics to avoid. Create a plan outlining when and how you'll engage with your mother, prioritizing your emotional well-being. Use this plan as a guide, revisiting it regularly to ensure it aligns with your evolving needs.

By embracing limited contact, you take a proactive step towards preserving your mental health while maintaining family connections. This approach empowers you to engage with intention, making interactions into opportunities for growth rather than sources of stress.

No Contact: When and How

Going no contact means completely severing ties, which often feels like a last resort. This decision is not taken lightly, as it involves ending all forms of communication with someone who played a pivotal role in your life. This cessation can lead to profound emotional relief and healing, providing space to rediscover your identity away from the shadows of manipulation and control. For many, this step is necessary for breaking free from cycles of emotional abuse and reclaiming personal peace. However, it also brings challenges, such as the potential for guilt and the complexities of grieving an ongoing relationship. The absence of contact might leave you grappling with loss, even as you gain autonomy and clarity.

Certain indicators suggest that going no contact is necessary for your well-being. Repeated boundary violations signal a disregard for your needs, a pattern that can erode your mental health over time. Escalating emotional or psychological harm, such as persistent anxiety or depression, might also indicate it's time to consider this step. When interactions with your mother consistently result in distress or self-doubt, the relationship becomes a source of harm rather than support. Recognizing these signs requires self-awareness and honesty about the impact on your life. It comes down to acknowledging the reality of your circumstances and prioritizing your emotional safety.

Implementing no contact involves several steps, each requiring careful consideration and planning. Start by informing close friends or allies of your decision. Their support will be invaluable, providing reassurance and perspective during this transition. Next, prepare for potential backlash or guilt. It's not uncommon to experience second thoughts or pressure from family members who may not understand your choice. Anticipating these feelings allows you to handle them with resilience. You might also face attempts from your mother to reestablish contact, using guilt or manipulation as tools. Establish a plan for how to respond, or not respond, to these attempts, reinforcing your boundaries.

Here is an example of a woman who found personal growth after deciding to go no contact. After years of enduring emotional abuse, Ann realized the toll it was taking on her mental health. Despite initial feelings of guilt, she informed her close friends and prepared for her mother's reaction. With their support, Ann blocked her mother's number and ceased all communication. In the following months, she experienced a newfound sense of freedom and peace. Without the constant barrage of negativity, she began to see herself more clearly, developing greater self-worth and confidence. This decision allowed her to rebuild her life, focusing on nurturing and reciprocal relationships.

Experts often highlight the psychological benefits of going no contact. It can lead to significant improvements in mental health, as the absence of toxic interactions reduces stress and anxiety. By eliminating the source of emotional harm, individuals create space for healing and personal growth. This decision can also empower you to establish healthier relationships, free from the patterns of manipulation and control. However, experts also caution that going no contact is not a panacea for past trauma. It is a step towards healing, but the process of recovery involves ongoing self-reflection and development. Seeking professional support can provide additional guidance and coping strategies, ensuring you manage this transition with confidence and clarity.

Dealing with Flying Monkeys

In the dynamics between narcissistic mothers and their daughters, the concept of "flying monkeys" emerges, painting a vivid picture of how enablers operate. These individuals are often manipulated to act on behalf of the narcissist, amplifying their agenda and creating a network of influence that extends beyond direct interactions. Flying monkeys can be family members, friends, or acquaintances who unknowingly, or sometimes knowingly, support the narcissist's behavior. They may carry messages, spread misinformation, or pressure you to reconcile, all while maintaining the appearance of neutrality. It's a subtle yet powerful tactic that allows the narcissist to maintain control without direct confrontation. The role of flying monkeys is to deflect attention from the narcissist's actions, making you question your perceptions and experiences. This can lead to further isolation, as you may feel that even those around you are aligned with the narcissist's perspective. Understanding this dynamic is very important in navigating your interactions and protecting your mental well-being.

Flying monkeys employ various tactics to manipulate and control the narrative. One common strategy is spreading misinformation, sowing seeds of doubt and confusion. They may distort facts or present a skewed version of events, painting you as the antagonist in the story. This can leave you questioning your reality and the validity of your feelings. Another tactic involves pressuring you for reconciliation, often under the guise of concern or maintaining family harmony. They might urge you to "forgive and forget," dismissing the emotional damage caused by the narcissist. Their words can carry a veneer of reasonableness, appealing to your desire for peace, but ultimately serving the narcissist's interests. The pressure to conform to their narrative can be overwhelming, especially when it comes from multiple sources. It's essential to recognize these tactics for what they are: attempts to undermine your autonomy and reinforce the narcissist's control.

To effectively manage interactions with flying monkeys, setting firm boundaries is paramount. Clearly articulate what topics are off-limits and how you prefer to communicate. This establishes a framework that limits their influence and reinforces your autonomy. If direct communication proves challenging, consider using neutral parties as intermediaries. This can help diffuse tension and prevent misunderstandings, allowing you to maintain control over the narrative. Another strategy is to remain calm and composed during interactions. Flying monkeys often thrive on emotional reactions, using them to justify their actions or escalate the situation. By responding with measured calmness, you deprive them of the fuel needed to perpetuate conflict. It's also important to document interactions, keeping a record of conversations and incidents. This provides a tangible reference point, reinforcing your reality against any attempts to distort it.

Here is an example that is common. A family member, acting as a flying monkey, approaches you with claims about a recent disagreement with your mother. They insist that your mother is deeply hurt and urge you to make amends. Recognizing this as a manipulation tactic, you calmly assert your boundaries, stating that you're willing to discuss the issue only when both parties are prepared to communicate respectfully. By refusing to engage in their narrative, you maintain control over the situation. Alternatively, imagine a conversation where a flying monkey tries to provoke a reaction by recounting exaggerated tales of your mother's suffering. Instead of reacting defensively, you choose to disengage, stating, "I appreciate your concern, but I'd prefer not to discuss this right now." This approach not only diffuses potential conflict but also reinforces your autonomy, demonstrating that you will not be swayed by external pressure.

Managing interactions with flying monkeys requires a blend of awareness, strategy, and resolve. Their influence can be pervasive, but by recognizing their tactics and asserting your boundaries, you can reclaim your narrative and reinforce your mental well-being. It's about maintaining your perspective amidst the noise, ensuring that your voice remains strong and clear in the face of manipulation.

Handling Family Gatherings

Family gatherings often bring a tumult of emotions, especially when maneuvering through the treacherous waters of narcissistic dynamics. These events, meant to be joyful, can become arenas of tension and psychological strain. You might find yourself walking on eggshells, anticipating the next subtle jab or backhanded compliment. The room feels charged with unspoken expectations and unresolved conflicts, each interaction potentially a trigger for confrontation. The emotional and psychological difficulties posed by such gatherings are about managing your feelings and navigating the complex web of family dynamics. It requires you to stay balanced amidst swirling emotions.

Preparation is your best defense when facing these gatherings. Setting personal goals can provide focus, helping you decide what you wish to achieve or avoid during the event. Perhaps your goal is simply to maintain a sense of calm or to enjoy a few genuine interactions. Whatever it is, having a clear objective can ground you, offering a touchstone when the atmosphere becomes overwhelming. Planning an exit strategy is equally important. Knowing how and when to leave, should tensions rise, offers a sense of control and safety. This might mean driving separately or having a friend on standby, ready to call you away if needed. Such plans are helpful in preserving your peace of mind.

Once at the gathering, managing interactions requires a blend of strategy and composure. Deep breathing or grounding exercises can help maintain your calm, offering a momentary refuge amidst the chaos. These techniques, simple yet effective, allow you to reset your emotional state, ensuring that you respond rather than react. Another useful approach is sticking to neutral conversation topics. Discussing the weather, shared interests, or current events can deflect attention from more contentious subjects. These neutral zones create a buffer, keeping interactions light and less emotionally charged. They allow you to engage without opening the door to deeper, potentially hurtful discussions.

Think os a scenario where you successfully navigate a tense family dinner. The atmosphere is thick with unspoken grievances; you are starting to get triggered by your mother's seemingly innocent comments that have a much deeper, darker meaning for you, but you focus on your goal to enjoy the evening with minimal conflict. You engage in conversations about shared memories, steering clear of topics that have previously sparked arguments. You refuse to take the bait and react to your mother's insinuations, double entendre, and overt jabs. During dinner, you notice a sibling acting like a flying monkey, trying to draw you into a heated debate. Instead of taking the bait, you excuse yourself to check on dessert, using the break to practice a few grounding breaths. This brief pause allows you to return to the table composed, ready to steer the conversation back to safer waters.

In another scenario, imagine having a supporting ally within the family context. A cousin, aware of the dynamics, quietly aligns with you. Together, you create a small, supportive bubble within the larger gathering. You share a knowing glance when tensions rise, offering silent solidarity. This connection becomes a lifeline, reminding you that you are not alone in handling the complexities of your mothers narcissism. Such alliances, often unspoken, are powerful. They provide reassurance and a sense of belonging, even in challenging environments. These scenarios exemplify how preparation and strategic interaction can transform a potentially fraught gathering into an event of manageable complexities.

Each family gathering is unique, a blend of personalities and histories that shape its dynamics. Yet, with thoughtful preparation and practiced strategies, you can get through these events with confidence and grace. While the challenges are real, they also present opportunities for growth and understanding. By approaching gatherings with clear goals, practiced techniques, and a focus on maintaining your peace, you reclaim your agency within the family narrative.

Protecting Your Mental Health

In the dynamics of family interactions, particularly with narcissistic mothers, safeguarding your mental health takes precedence. The importance of this cannot be overstated. Engaging with family should not come at the expense of your emotional resilience. It is crucial to ensure that your mental fortitude remains intact, preventing psychological harm that prolonged exposure to toxic dynamics can inflict. Emotional resilience is your armor, protection against the negative energy that often accompanies interactions with a narcissistic mother. Without it, the risk of internalizing harmful behaviors and criticisms increases, potentially leading to anxiety, depression, or a diminished sense of self-worth. When you prioritize your mental health, you lay the foundation for a life where you thrive despite the legacy of growing up with a narcissistic mother.

Maintaining mental health during ongoing interactions requires a proactive approach. Regular therapy or counseling sessions offer a safe space to explore feelings and develop coping strategies. These sessions can give you the tools to understand complex emotions, reinforcing your capacity to handle familial challenges. Equally important is developing a support network of friends or peers who understand your experiences. This network acts as a sounding board, offering empathy and perspective when family interactions become overwhelming. Their support can validate your feelings, reminding you that you are not alone in this struggle and that your experiences are legitimate. Together, therapy and community form a robust support system, strengthening your mental health resilience.

Stress management and emotional regulation techniques are invaluable for adult daughters in maintaining their mental health when interacting with their narcissistic mothers. Mindfulness and meditation practices can anchor you in the present, reducing the emotional upheaval that past encounters may trigger. These practices cultivate a sense of inner peace, allowing you to approach situations with calm and clarity. Engaging in physical activity or hobbies provides a healthy outlet for stress, channeling energy into positive pursuits that rejuvenate the mind and body. Whether it's a brisk walk, going for a bike ride, hitting the gym, or gardening, these activities create a healthy place where you can unwind and recharge. They remind you of the joys and passions that define you, separate from the gravitational pull of your narcissistic mother and family tensions.

Testimonials from those who have successfully protected their mental health offer valuable insights. Erica recounts how mindfulness became her refuge amidst the chaos of family drama. By dedicating time each day to meditation, she found a way to center herself, reducing stress and enhancing her emotional resilience. This practice allowed her to engage with her mother from a place of strength, maintaining her boundaries and sense of self. Experts emphasize the importance of these strategies, noting that consistent self-care and emotional regulation are key to maintaining mental well-being in challenging family environments. They advise establishing routines that prioritize your needs, ensuring that self-care becomes a non-negotiable part of your life.

As you work through these complex dynamics, remember that mental health is not a luxury, it's a necessity. Prioritizing it empowers you to engage with your mother on your terms, without losing yourself in the process. By integrating these practices into your life, you create a protective barrier that fortifies your emotional resilience, allowing you to thrive despite the challenges. The path to mental well-being is ongoing, requiring intention, patience, and dedication, but each step taken reinforces your capacity to live authentically and joyfully. As you continue this exploration, know that the path to healing and empowerment is within reach, guided by the strength you cultivate within.

With these insights, you can better face interactions with your mother, armed with strategies to protect your mental health and foster resilience. In the next chapter, you will find learn strategies for reclaiming personal power and understanding that the journey of healing is both profound and transformative.

Chapter 9
Overcoming Common Objections

You are standing at the edge of a forest, where the path ahead is obscured by dense fog. You know you must move forward, but the uncertainty of what lies beyond the mist keeps you rooted in place. This is the essence of the fear of change, a potent blend of the unknown and an innate attachment to what is familiar, even if that familiarity is steeped in discomfort. For daughters of narcissistic mothers, this fear can be particularly paralyzing. The idea of stepping into a new chapter of life, away from ingrained patterns, feels risky and very uncomfortable. Change challenges the comfort of predictability and the control that comes with knowing what to expect, even when those expectations are rooted in dysfunction.

The fear of losing control is a significant barrier to embracing change. Growing up, you might have felt powerless as your mother dictated the narrative of your life. This lack of agency created a reliance on the known, where even harmful patterns offer a semblance of control and comfort amidst chaos. The comfort in these familiar patterns can be deceptive, providing a false sense of security. Change demands that you relinquish this control and venture into uncharted territory, which can trigger anxiety and resistance. However, this very act of letting go opens the door to personal growth and the discovery of new strengths. Embracing change can reveal capabilities you never knew you possessed, fostering resilience and adaptability. Each step forward offers opportunities for personal development, expanding your horizons beyond the constraints of your past.

Managing the fear of change involves utilizing strategies that empower you to face and overcome these challenges. Begin by visualizing the positive outcomes that change can bring. Imagining a life where you feel empowered and self-assured can provide the motivation to take that first step. Gradual exposure to new situations can also ease the transition, allowing you to build confidence incrementally. Start small, perhaps by exploring a new hobby or changing your daily routine. These small acts of courage accumulate, reinforcing your ability to handle larger changes with grace.

Consider the story of Lisa, who spent years in an unrewarding career shaped by her mother's expectations. One day, she decided to pursue her passion for interior design, a field she had always admired from afar. The transition was daunting, filled with self-doubt and the fear of failure. Yet, as she immersed herself in creative projects, she discovered a satisfaction and joy she hadn't known before. Her career shift brought professional fulfillment and strengthened her sense of identity, allowing her to step out of the shadows of her mother's influence.

Another example is Sarah, who decided to move to a new city after feeling stifled by the constraints of her environment. The move was a leap into the unknown, filled with both excitement and fear. However, the change allowed her to redefine her life on her terms, away from her mother's expectations that had previously dictated her choices. In the new city, she found a community that supported her growth and encouraged her authenticity.

The experience taught her that change, while initially intimidating, could lead to unexpected opportunities and a richer, more fulfilling life.

Visualizing Change

Take a moment to close your eyes and envision a future where you have embraced change. Picture yourself in a place that represents growth and fulfillment, surrounded by elements that bring you joy and peace. What do you see? What emotions surface? Use this visualization as motivation to take steps toward realizing this vision. This exercise can serve as a powerful tool to overcome the initial fear, reinforcing the belief that change is not something to fear but a pathway to a more empowered and authentic self.

Overcoming the Triggering of Past Memories

It's a sunny afternoon, and the smell of fresh-cut grass wafts through the air as you stroll through the park. Suddenly, a song plays from a nearby radio, tugging you back to a moment you'd rather forget, a birthday party from years ago, where your mother's sharp words left an indelible mark. Triggers like these, often mundane and unexpected, can stir up memories you thought were long buried. Specific dates or anniversaries can also remind us of past hurts, making even the most joyous occasions feel heavy. Interactions with certain people, perhaps someone who resembles your mother in tone or temperament, can also evoke those familiar pangs of anxiety. These triggers, though varied, share a common thread: they transport you to emotional states that are challenging to deal with.

Managing these triggered memories requires intentional effort and compassion. Grounding exercises can help you stay present when past memories threaten to overwhelm you. Simple techniques, like focusing on the sensation of your feet on the ground or the rhythm of your breath, can create a buffer between the present and the past. Cognitive reframing is another powerful tool. You can reduce their emotional grip by challenging and reshaping the narratives associated with these memories. For instance, you might remind yourself that the hurtful words spoken long ago were not a reflection of your worth but rather a projection of your mother's unresolved issues. This reframing can transform a painful memory into an opportunity for self-validation and growth.

In moments of heightened emotion, self-compassion becomes your greatest resource. It's easy to judge yourself harshly for feeling triggered, questioning why these memories still hold power. Instead, acknowledge your emotional responses with kindness. Understand that these reactions are natural, given your history. Practicing self-care rituals can further support this process. Whether it's a warm bath, a walk in nature, or simply allowing yourself a moment of stillness, these acts of self-care reinforce the message that you are worthy of love and understanding. By treating yourself with gentleness, you create a safe space to process and release the emotions tied to your past.

A great example of how self-care can help is seen in Laura's story. Laura found strength and peace in taking fitness classes and committing to her health. Each cardio circuit she completed became a way to express the emotions that words couldn't capture. Laura discovered new insights and healing by channeling her memories into her workouts. This outlet of expression allowed her to reframe her past, transforming it into a source of strength rather than pain. Another example is Kelly, who embraced mindfulness as a path to emotional regulation. Through daily meditation, she learned to observe her triggers without judgment, gaining the clarity needed to navigate her emotional landscape. This practice helped Kelly cultivate a sense of inner peace, empowering her to face the echos of her mother's dysfunction with a healthy perspective.

Memory Mapping

Take a moment to engage in a memory-mapping exercise. Find a quiet space and sit comfortably. Close your eyes and breathe deeply. When you feel ready, allow your mind to wander to a memory that often triggers you. Instead of focusing on the emotions, visualize the details surrounding the memory. What were the colors, sounds, or smells? Write these down, creating a map of sensory experiences. Next, identify a positive memory and map its details. Compare the two maps, noting differences and similarities. This exercise offers a new perspective, helping you understand your triggers and reinforcing that your past does not define your present.

Simplifying Complex Emotions

Emotions are rarely straightforward. Often, they're tangled like a ball of yarn, each thread representing a different feeling, all knotted together. For daughters who grew up with narcissistic mothers, this challenge is even more pronounced. For example, you might feel mixed emotions toward family members. Love, resentment, obligation, and guilt can coexist, competing for attention and leaving you unsure how to respond. This emotional confusion extends to personal desires and needs. You might struggle to identify what you truly want as the lines between your wishes and those imposed by your mother blur. This internal chaos can make it difficult to trust your feelings or make decisions, trapping you in a state of inaction.

Untangling these emotions requires deliberate effort and introspection. One effective technique is emotion journaling. By writing down your feelings, you can begin to see patterns and gain clarity. Journaling allows you to externalize your emotions, turning an abstract whirlwind into something tangible. As you write, try to identify the primary emotions beneath the surface reactions. For instance, anger often masks fear and frustration, and sadness could be hiding disappointment. By recognizing these underlying feelings, you can address the root causes rather than just the symptoms. This exercise helps you understand what you're feeling and why you're feeling it, paving the way for deeper emotional clarity and insight.

The benefits of achieving emotional clarity are profound. When you understand your emotions, you can communicate more effectively. This understanding enhances your emotional intelligence, enabling you to approach relationships with greater ease. Improved communication skills mean you're better able to express your needs and set boundaries, which in turn promotes healthier interactions. Emotional clarity also leads to better decision-making. When you're clear about your feelings, you can make choices that align with your true self rather than being swayed by external pressures. This alignment leads to authenticity and confidence, empowering you to live a life that reflects your values and desires.

For example, let's look at Rachel and her story. Rachel spent years feeling conflicted about her relationship with her mother. Therapy provided a space for her to unpack these emotions. Through guided sessions, she learned to separate her mother's expectations from her own desires. This clarity allowed Rachel to redefine her boundaries and voice her needs without fear. Similarly, Renee found emotional clarity through meditation. By practicing mindfulness, she learned to observe her emotions without judgment, gaining insight into her responses. This practice helped her identify the primary emotions driving her behavior, sit with them, and feel compassion for herself. Renee was able to make the connection between her constant fear of abandonment and low self-esteem to the abuse she suffered her whole life from her her mother's need to be the center of attention. This connection and realization allowed Renee to move forward and approach her relationships with understanding and compassion.

Finding Time for Personal Growth

In the whirlwind of daily life, carving out time for personal growth often feels like an uphill battle. The demands of work, family obligations, and social commitments can leave you feeling stretched thin, with little energy left for self-improvement. It's easy to become overcommitted, prioritizing the needs of others over your own. This pattern, often ingrained from a young age, can lead to neglecting self-care, as you're conditioned to believe that your worth is tied to how much you can give. Yet personal growth is central to building a fulfilling life where your goals and dreams take center stage. Recognizing and breaking free from the cycle of overcommitment is the first step toward reclaiming your time.

To make room for personal development, start by setting small, manageable goals. These goals act as stepping stones, leading you toward larger aspirations without overwhelming you. Begin with something simple, like dedicating ten minutes each day to read a chapter of a book related to your interests or spending a few minutes in meditation. Following through with this and giving yourself 10 minutes daily to read re-inforces your worth and silences the inner critic in your mind. These seemingly minor commitments can accumulate, creating momentum and creating a sense of achievement. Utilizing time-blocking techniques can also be incredibly effective. You make a structured routine that prioritizes self-improvement alongside other responsibilities by allocating specific time slots for personal growth activities in your calendar. This approach helps prevent the day from slipping away without accomplishing what matters to you.

Consistency is key to personal development. Regular engagement in growth activities ensures sustained progress, allowing you to build upon each small success. Creating a routine dedicated to personal development tasks can help embed these activities into your daily life. Whether it's setting aside early mornings for reflection or using lunch breaks for learning a new skill, finding pockets of time throughout the day can transform how you manage your growth. Consistency not only reinforces habits but also nurtures a mindset that values continuous learning and self-discovery.

Take the story of Emily, who found clarity and purpose by waking up an hour earlier each day. She used this quiet time to practice yoga and set intentions, which helped her stay focused on her personal goals amidst her busy schedule. This practice allowed Emily to reconnect with herself, providing a foundation for deeper personal growth. Meanwhile, Taylor, a busy professional, started using her lunch breaks to learn a new language. What began as a casual interest turned into a passion, enriching her personal and professional life. These examples illustrate how even the busiest individuals can find time for growth, leading to a more balanced and fulfilling life.

Time-Blocking Exercise

One of the most effective exercises I have come across is a simple one, and it really makes a difference. To help integrate personal growth into your routine, try this exercise: list three personal development goals you wish to pursue. These don't have to be major things; they can be, but they don't have to be. They can be as simple as getting to bed before 10 pm every night, taking a hot bath over the weekend, and going for a walk once this week. Next, look at your weekly schedule and identify specific time slots where you can dedicate time to each goal. Block these times in your calendar, treating them as non-negotiable appointments with yourself. Reflect on how keeping these little commitments to yourself impacts your sense of fulfillment and progress over the coming weeks. This exercise encourages intentional growth, improves self-image, and reinforces the importance of valuing personal development.

Recognizing and Refuting Self-Blame

In the shadow of a narcissistic mother, self-blame is a constant, unwelcome companion. As a child, you may have absorbed her manipulative tactics like a sponge, internalizing guilt that was never yours to carry. When her unreasonable expectations went unmet, the blame inevitably fell on you, fostering a persistent doubt that questioned your every move. This pattern often begins with subtle criticisms that slowly erode your confidence. Over time, these seeds of doubt can grow into a belief system where you feel responsible for her discontent and shortcomings, leaving you perpetually questioning your worth and decisions.

Recognizing these patterns of self-blame is a critical step in breaking free from their hold. One effective technique is documenting the instance when you feel self-blame. You can identify recurring themes and triggers by noting moments when you feel guilty or at fault. This practice helps illuminate situations where self-blame arises, allowing you to see it for what it truly is: a learned response rather than a reflection of reality. Analyzing past incidents with a discerning eye can also reveal the origins of these feelings. Look for patterns where you were unjustly held accountable for things beyond your control. Understanding these patterns can provide clarity, reinforcing that your guilt does not define you.

To release self-blame, adopting strategies that challenge and transform these ingrained beliefs is essential. Practicing self-forgiveness exercises can be liberating. Allow yourself the grace to acknowledge mistakes, understanding that they are part of the human experience, not indictments of your character. Engaging in positive self-talk can further diminish the grip of self-blame. Replace negative thoughts with affirmations that reinforce your worth and capabilities. Phrases like "I am enough" or "I am doing my best" can be powerful antidotes to self-critical narratives. These affirmations help rewire your brain, supporting a mindset that values self-compassion and resilience over perfection.

Ellie's story demonstrates just how powerful this can be. Ellie committed to do the work and entered therapy with a skilled therapist. Ellie explained what her life was like growing up with a narcissistic mother and the ripples her childhood experience still has on her day-to-day life. Ellie and her therapist decided Ellie needed to embrace self-acceptance. Her therapist guided her in exploring the roots of her self-blame, helping her understand how her mother's words had shaped her self-image. Through this introspection, Ellie began challenging these internalized messages, replacing them with affirmations celebrating her strengths and individuality. Over time, she discovered a newfound sense of peace and confidence, free from the weight of unjust guilt. Another example is Candace, who used daily affirmations to combat her negative self-perception. By consistently reinforcing positive beliefs about herself, she gradually dismantled the self-blame that had long overshadowed her life.

The process of recognizing and refuting self-blame can be transformative, shifting the focus from past burdens to future possibilities. By understanding the origins of these feelings and employing targeted strategies to counteract them, you can reclaim your narrative and embrace a more empowered self. As you do this work, remember that you are not alone, and learning to be more self-compassionate and accepting is a testament to your strength and resilience. Recognizing your inherent worth and allowing yourself the freedom to grow and thrive without the constraints of past judgments or expectations is immensely powerful.

In this chapter, we have explored the common objections and barriers you may encounter on your path to healing. By addressing fears, managing triggers, simplifying emotions, finding time for growth, and refuting self-blame, you set the stage for transformation. As you move forward, prepare to engage with strategies for developing resilience and building a life that aligns with your true self.

Chapter 10
Lifelong Healing and Support

In the quiet moments just before dawn, while the world is still wrapped in darkness, you may find yourself awake, reflecting on your life. The silence offers a rare opportunity to consider your path forward, free from the chaotic demands of the day. In these introspective moments, the idea of a lifelong healing plan takes root. This plan is a living blueprint that grows and evolves alongside you. It is a personalized map tailored to your unique experiences and needs, guiding you toward sustained healing and growth. Creating such a plan is necessary because your journey is unlike anyone else's; it requires a strategy that honors your individuality and adapts to life's inevitable changes.

The importance of a personalized healing plan cannot be overstated. It is a reflection of your distinct experiences, addressing the specific wounds and challenges you face as the daughter of a narcissistic mother. A one-size-fits-all approach won't suffice when dealing with the complexities of emotional neglect and manipulation. Your plan should be flexible and ready to adapt as circumstances shift and new insights emerge. It must account for the nuances of your life, allowing you to set realistic goals that align with your values and aspirations. By focusing on your unique needs, you empower yourself to progress confidently and clearly.

To develop a comprehensive healing plan, begin by identifying your long-term goals and milestones. These are the aspirations that inspire you, the achievements that signify progress along your path. Reflect on what you hope to accomplish, both emotionally and practically. Ask yourself what healing looks like for you and what steps you need to take to get there. Once your goals are clear, break them down into smaller, manageable milestones. These milestones are markers, guiding your efforts and marking moments of triumph along the way. Regular self-assessment and reflection are integral to this process, allowing you to track your progress and adjust as needed. By continually evaluating your journey, you ensure your plan remains relevant and effective, adapting to your evolving needs and circumstances.

Incorporating various healing modalities into your plan can enhance its effectiveness, providing a holistic approach to your well-being. Consider integrating therapy, whether through traditional talk therapy or more specialized methods like cognitive behavioral therapy (CBT) or Acceptance and Commitment Therapy (ACT). These therapeutic modalities offer valuable tools for processing emotions and restructuring negative thought patterns. Meditation and mindfulness practices can further support your healing, encouraging present-moment awareness and creating a sense of inner peace. Creative outlets, such as art or writing, allow for self-expression and emotional release, helping to articulate feelings that may be difficult to verbalize. Physical activities like yoga or tai chi promote physical health and emotional balance, offering a way to connect with your body and cultivate resilience.

Take, for example, the story of Ellen, who blended therapy and community service into her healing plan. After years of feeling disconnected from herself and others, Ellen found solace and purpose in volunteering at a local women's shelter. This service became a cornerstone of her healing journey, providing a sense of belonging and fulfillment. She related to these women, some of whom had also had narcissistic mothers, and developed a great sense of confidence and pride through her work with these women. In therapy, Ellen worked to untangle the emotional threads and all the scars from her mother's narcissism, gaining insights that informed her volunteer work. Each session helped her build confidence, which she channeled into her interactions with those she helped and befriended at the shelter. It gave Ellen a real sense of belonging and acceptance, something she had never received from her mother. Ellen's plan exemplifies the power of combining personal growth with community engagement, illustrating how healing can extend beyond the self to impact the wider world.

Another example is Samantha, who crafted a healing plan focused on creative expression and mindfulness. As a pianist, Samantha had always found comfort in her art, yet she had never considered it part of her healing process. Samantha discovered a renewed sense of purpose and joy by integrating regular music sessions into her plan. Alongside her creative pursuits, Samantha embraced mindfulness meditation, dedicating time each day to quiet reflection. This practice helped her cultivate a deeper connection with her emotions, allowing her to deal with life's challenges more easily. Samantha's plan demonstrates how creative expression and mindfulness can work in tandem, supporting emotional resilience and personal growth.

Crafting Your Healing Blueprint

Take some time to outline your own healing plan. Begin by writing down your long-term goals, considering what healing means to you personally.

Break these goals into smaller milestones, noting the steps you will take to achieve them. Reflect on the healing modalities that resonate with you, such as therapy, meditation, or creative pursuits, and consider how they can be integrated into your plan. Remember to include regular self-assessment and reflection, allowing your plan to evolve as you grow. Keep this blueprint in a place where you can revisit it often, using it as an outline and source of inspiration on your way to healing and empowerment.

As you start on this path, know that your healing plan is a testament to your commitment to yourself. It reflects your strength and resilience, a declaration that you are worthy of the peace and happiness you seek. Embrace the journey with an open heart, trusting in the process and your ability to create a life that honors your true self.

Finding Joy Beyond the Shadow

One very important thing that adult adults of narcissistic mothers can do to break free of the legacy of insecurity and self-doubt passed on by the mother is to find joyful activities.

Growing up with a narcissistic mother often leaves a daughter with a deep sense of confusion about her identity and worth. Narcissistic mothers typically exert an overbearing level of control, prioritizing their own needs and desires while dismissing or undermining their daughter's individuality. For adult daughters of such mothers, stepping out from under their mother's shadow is not an act of rebellion; it's an essential step toward reclaiming their happiness and independence. One powerful way to do this is by discovering and engaging in activities that bring joy, even when it triggers fear, insecurity, or resistance from the mother.

The Impact of Narcissistic Control

A narcissistic mother often sets the stage for her daughter's life by dictating her choices, dismissing her emotions, and undermining her self-worth. This control can stifle the daughter's natural curiosity and creativity, leaving her unsure of what truly makes her happy. In many cases, the daughter learns to prioritize her mother's needs and opinions over her own, becoming trapped in a cycle of seeking approval that is rarely given. As a result, even in adulthood, she will feel guilty or anxious about pursuing her own interests, fearing rejection, criticism, or manipulation.

Breaking free from this dynamic requires the adult daughter to take courageous steps toward self-discovery. One of the most transformative actions she can take is to explore activities that bring her joy. On the surface, these pursuits may seem to be hobbies, but they are acts of self-empowerment. By engaging in activities that resonate with her, the daughter begins to reconnect with her authentic self, independent of her mother's influence.

This process often involves trial and error. She may need to experiment with different hobbies, creative outlets, or social activities to uncover what truly excites and fulfills her. Whether it's playing tennis, reading books, dancing, hiking, or learning a new skill, these activities remind her that her worth is not tied to her mother's approval. They are opportunities to nurture her inner child and create a sense of autonomy and self-respect.

Confronting Fear and Insecurity

For many daughters of narcissistic mothers, stepping into this space of joy and independence is not without its challenges. It can be incredibly difficult and create anxiety and fear. This can be overwhelming and partly explains why so many adult daughters can never fully separate from their mothers and go on to lead a healthy, fulfilling life. Narcissistic mothers are often highly manipulative and may react negatively to their daughter's attempts at autonomy. They may belittle her interests, dismiss her accomplishments, or use guilt to pull her back into their sphere of control.

This manipulation can trigger deep-seated fears, insecurities, and feelings of inadequacy. The daughter may question whether she deserves happiness or if pursuing her interests is worth the potential backlash. She may also struggle with feelings of anxiety, as breaking away from her mother's control represents uncharted emotional territory.

However, it is precisely in facing these fears that the daughter begins to heal. Each time she chooses to prioritize her joy over her mother's expectations, she reinforces her sense of independence and self-worth. Over time, this strengthens her ability to set boundaries, resist manipulation, and trust her instincts.

The Power of Courage

Engaging in joyful activities despite fear is an act of courage for a daughter of a narcissistic mother. It's a declaration that her happiness matters and that she is more than a reflection of her mother's desires. This courage often builds slowly, starting with small steps: attending a class, carving out time for a favorite hobby, or spending time with supportive friends who encourage her growth.

The more she invests in these activities, the more she experiences the intrinsic rewards of joy and fulfillment. These moments of happiness, however small at first, become powerful motivators. They provide a sense of balance and grounding, helping her respond to the emotional challenges of disentangling herself from her mother's influence.

Long-Term Benefits

Finding and engaging in joyful activities has long-term benefits beyond immediate happiness. These pursuits help rebuild self-esteem, proving she is capable, creative, and deserving of pleasure. They also create opportunities for connection with others who share similar interests, cultivating a sense of community and belonging that may have been missing in her relationship with her mother.

Over time, these activities become a foundation for a more balanced and fulfilling life. They provide a sense of purpose and direction, helping the daughter move forward with clarity and confidence. As she grows more comfortable in her independence, she learns to trust her instincts and embrace her individuality, leaving behind the fear and self-doubt that once held her back.

Tips for Success

- **Start Small**: Begin with low-pressure activities that feel approachable, such as taking a walk in nature or trying a beginner's class.

- **Focus on Enjoyment**: Choose activities that genuinely interest you, rather than those that feel like obligations or a means to impress others.

- **Create Boundaries**: Protect your time and energy by setting firm boundaries with your mother and anyone who tries to undermine your efforts.

- **Seek Support**: Surround yourself with people who uplift and encourage you, whether it's friends, a support group, or a therapist.

- **Celebrate Progress**: Acknowledge and celebrate your successes, no matter how small. Every step forward is a victory.

For adult daughters of narcissistic mothers, finding joy through activities that resonate with their authentic selves is a vital part of moving on with their lives. It requires courage, persistence, and a willingness to face the discomfort of stepping out from under their mother's shadow. But the rewards, self-discovery, independence, and genuine happiness are worth every effort.

By prioritizing her own joy, the daughter reclaims her identity and sets a powerful example of determination and self-love. It's a road toward freedom, one step at a time, and every moment of joy is a reminder that she deserves a life of her own making.

Finding Hobbies and Activities

Finding hobbies and activities that resonate with your interests and goals can bring immense joy and fulfillment. To start this process, it's helpful to consider a few key criteria. Start by focusing on activities that align with your personal values, those that reflect your core beliefs, allow you to express your authentic self, and contribute positively to your overall well-being. Look for environments that provide an atmosphere of enjoyment and comfort, where you can engage without judgment or criticism, and where the experience feels relaxed and supportive.

Consider opportunities for engagement, such as classes, workshops, or groups, that allow you to connect with others with similar interests. These opportunities enhance your experience and encourage learning, growth, and a sense of belonging. Choose activities that positively challenge you, stimulate your creativity, or offer a sense of accomplishment. Engaging in hobbies that expose you to diverse perspectives or new ideas can broaden your understanding of the world and enrich your overall experience.

Practicality is another important factor. Make sure the activity is feasible and accessible within your schedule and budget and that the resources or materials needed are easy to obtain. Finally, prioritize activities that spark genuine excitement or curiosity. These should be pursuits you look forward to, whether you're participating in them independently or as part of a group.

As you explore hobbies and activities, remember that they offer more than just personal enjoyment; they provide opportunities for connection, self-discovery, and growth. Each new interest can lead to deeper insights about yourself and help you build a fulfilling life. They can help you develop and strengthen your sense of pride and confidence in your own abilities. Through active participation, you'll uncover what truly brings you joy and contribute to a richer, more vibrant version of yourself.

Accessing Expert Insights and Resources

Working with a professional who is an expert in the often crippling cascade of emotions that daughters of narcissistic mothers face can be extremely helpful. Your work with a therapist will focus on gaining a deeper understanding of yourself and the challenges you face and developing an actionable plan to get through these big, overwhelming emotions. Experts bring the latest research and therapeutic techniques to the table, providing evidence-based strategies tailored to your specific needs. This personalized advice isn't a one-size-fits-all solution but a customized approach that acknowledges your unique situation, making each step forward more meaningful.

Finding reputable experts and resources is a critical step in this journey of self-discovery and healing. Start by consulting licensed therapists and counselors who have extensive experience in dealing with narcissistic relationships and childhood emotional neglect. These professionals can offer insights rooted in psychological research and clinical practice, helping you unpack the intricacies of your experiences. Online platforms and directories often list qualified therapists, allowing you to read reviews and find someone who resonates with your needs. Additionally, academic journals and books by experts in the field provide a wealth of knowledge, offering in-depth analyses and practical advice. These resources are invaluable for those who seek a deeper understanding of the psychological dynamics at play. When choosing books or articles, look for works authored by respected psychologists or therapists, ensuring that the information is both credible and relevant to your situation.

Continuous learning and adaptation are vital components of personal growth. By staying informed and open to new ideas, you can evolve and adapt as you encounter new challenges. Attending workshops and conferences can be a powerful way to engage with the latest developments in psychology and therapy. These events provide opportunities to learn from experts, interact with peers, and gain hands-on experience with new techniques. Engaging with webinars and online courses can also be beneficial, offering flexibility and accessibility. These platforms allow you to explore a wide range of topics at your own pace, integrating new knowledge into your daily life. The key is to remain curious and willing to explore new approaches, recognizing that growth often comes from unexpected places.

Consider the story of Tia, who experienced a profound transformation through a specialized therapy program. After years of struggling with self-doubt and anxiety, Tia sought help from a therapist specializing in Eye Movement Desensitization and Reprocessing (EMDR). This innovative therapy helped her reprocess distressing memories, reducing their emotional intensity and allowing her to move forward with greater confidence. By embracing this specialized approach, Tia gained tools to manage her emotions more effectively, transforming her relationship with herself and others. Her experience illustrates the power of expert guidance in facilitating meaningful change, highlighting the importance of seeking out resources that align with your needs.

Another example is the impact of insights from a renowned self-help author on Emma's life. Emma, who felt trapped and crippled by the expectations set by her narcissistic mother, found solace in the writings of a psychologist known for her work on self-acceptance and personal growth. Emma gained a new perspective on her experiences through the author's books and seminars, learning to challenge the internalized beliefs that had held her back. The exercises and reflective prompts offered by the author encouraged Emma to explore her identity beyond the constraints of her upbringing. This newfound clarity empowered her to set boundaries and pursue her passions, giving her a sense of empowerment and self-worth.

Resource List: Exploring Expert Insights

1. Books: Seek out titles by psychologists and therapists specializing in narcissistic relationships and emotional neglect.

2. Therapists: Ask your physician to recommend licensed counselors who specialize in childhood trauma.

3. Workshops and Conferences: Explore events hosted by organizations like the American Psychological Association (APA) or local mental health associations.

4. Webinars and Online Courses: Platforms like Coursera or Udemy offer courses on psychology and personal development, allowing you to learn from experts worldwide.

Accessing expert insights and resources can deepen your understanding and enrich your healing process. As you explore these avenues, remember that the process is as much about growth as it is about discovery. With each new insight, you build a foundation of knowledge that supports your continued evolution, empowering you to navigate life's challenges with resilience and grace.

Conclusion

As you reach the end of this book, take a moment to reflect on the intricate dynamics of relationships with narcissistic mothers and the profound impact these relationships have on daughters. We've explored the subtleties of narcissistic behavior, from the disruptive family roles to the emotional manipulation that leaves a lasting imprint. Understanding these dynamics is a must in unraveling the web of confusion and pain that stems from such relationships.

Your path to health is about understanding these patterns and actively engaging in the process of reclaiming your life. From the initial recognition of narcissistic traits to the implementation of healing strategies, each step is a pivotal move toward empowerment. Breaking free from the dysfunctional legacy of a narcissistic upbringing requires dedication, but the reward is a healthier, more fulfilling life. This book has provided specific, real-life solutions to start this transformation.

As you reflect on the chapters, remember the key takeaways that have guided you. Recognizing your mother's narcissistic behaviors and their impact is the first step toward liberation. Establishing boundaries is not just about saying no; it's about defining your space and respecting your needs. Embracing your self-identity means identifying what truly matters to you, separate from the expectations imposed and implied by your mother. Personal growth is the ultimate goal of nurturing your self-esteem and building a life aligned with your values.

Your ability to overcome past challenges and create a brighter future is within reach. The stories of transformation and growth shared in this book inspire and motivate. They illustrate that change is possible and that you are not alone in your struggles. Each narrative reminds you of your strength and the boundless potential that lies ahead.

Now, I encourage you to take action. The strategies and exercises discussed are tools for your daily life. Implement them with intention, and let them guide you toward ongoing personal development and healing. This commitment to growth is lifelong, but each step forward builds resilience and empowerment.

To support you further, consider exploring additional resources. A companion website or community forum can provide a space for connection and continued learning. Books and academic articles offer deeper insights and broader perspectives on the topics we've covered. These resources serve as extensions of this book, offering continued guidance and support.

Acknowledging your courage is essential. Facing the past and taking steps toward healing requires bravery and grit. I am deeply grateful for your trust and for allowing me to guide you through this process. Your willingness to confront difficult truths and embrace change is a testament to your strength.

As you continue on your path, hold onto a sense of hope and encouragement. Investing in yourself encourages self-discovery and empowerment, filled with opportunities for growth and renewal. Embrace each moment with an open heart, knowing that a healthier, more authentic life is within your grasp. You have the power to shape your future, and I hope this book has given you the confidence and tools to do so. Remember, you are not defined by your past but by the strength and courage you bring into your future.

References

Adult daughters of narcissistic mothers. (n.d.). *New Harbinger.* Retrieved from https://www.newharbinger.com/9781648480096/adult-daughters-of-narcissistic-mothers/

A daughter's story of one hell of a narcissistic mother. (n.d.). *Narcissist Family Files.* Retrieved from https://narcissistfamilyfiles.com/category/the-narcissist-family-files/a-daughters-story-of-one-hell-of-a-narcissist-mother/

Attachment-based therapy explained: Techniques and approaches. (n.d.). *Attachment Project.* Retrieved from https://www.attachmentproject.com/psychology/attachment-based-therapy/

Cognitive restructuring: Techniques and examples. (n.d.) *Healthline.* Retrieved from https://www.healthline.com/health/cognitive-restructuring

Childhood emotional neglect: Signs, effects, and how to heal. (n.d.). *Medical News Today*. Retrieved from https://www.medicalnewstoday.com/articles/childhood-emotional-neglect

Childhood emotional neglect therapy in Madison, Guilford, and beyond. (n.d.). *Realms of Life Counseling*. Retrieved from https://realmsoflifecounseling.com/childhood-emotional-neglect

Children of narcissistic parents: Effects, healing, and more. (n.d.). *Healthline*. Retrieved from https://www.healthline.com/health/mental-health/children-of-narcissistic-parents

Consequences of child abuse and neglect. (n.d.). *National Center for Biotechnology Information (NCBI)*. Retrieved from https://www.ncbi.nlm.nih.gov/books/NBK195987/

4 types of gaslighting in families. (n.d.). *Psychology Today*. Retrieved from https://www.psychologytoday.com/intl/blog/childhood-emotional-neglect/202209/4-types-gaslighting-in-families

Grandiose and vulnerable narcissism from the perspective of others. (n.d.). *ScienceDirect*. Retrieved from https://www.sciencedirect.com/science/article/pii/S0191886912001912#:~:text=Vulnerable%20narcissism%20(VN)%20i s%20characterized,immodesty%2C%20exhibitionism%2C%20and%20aggression.

Grey rock method: What it is and how to use it effectively. (n.d.). *Medical News Today*. Retrieved from https://www.medicalnewstoday.com/articles/grey-rock

Healing from a narcissistic parent: Steps to recovery. (n.d.). *CircleSup*. Retrieved from https://circlesup.com/blog/healing-from-a-narcissistic-parent/

Healing from trauma: How community helps survivors. (n.d.). *Stand Together*. Retrieved from https://standtogether.org/stories/strong-safe-communities/healing-from-trauma-how-survivors-find-resilience-through-community-support#:~:text=Healing%20trauma%20through%20community%20support,essential%20support%20that%20eases%20isolation.

How to find a narcissistic abuse support group. (n.d.). *Verywell Mind*. Retrieved from https://www.verywellmind.com/how-to-find-a-narcissistic-abuse-support-group-5271477

How to recover from a narcissistic mother (for the daughters). (n.d.). *Medium*. Retrieved from https://medium.com/@olaradka/how-to-recover-from-a-narcissistic-mother-for-the-daughters-9e7c1574eb2a

How to validate yourself using dialectical behavior therapy. (n.d.). *Psychology Today*. Retrieved from https://www.psychologytoday.com/us/blog/the-addiction-connection/202406/how-to-validate-yourself-using-dialectical-behavior-therapy

I had no idea my mother was a narcissist until it was too late. (n.d.). *Amanda Robins Psychotherapy*. Retrieved from https://www.amandarobinspsychotherapy.com.au/articles/raised-by-narcissists-healing-for-daughters-of-narcissistic-mothers

Narcissistic mothers: The effects on their daughters. (n.d.). *Simply Psychology*. Retrieved from https://www.simplypsychology.org/daughters-of-narcissistic-mothers.html

Narcissistic mothers: The effects on their daughters and how to heal. (n.d.). *PsychCentral*. Retrieved from https://psychcentral.com/disorders/narcissistic-personality-disorder/narcissistic-mothers-the-long-term-effects-on-their-daughters

Once I stopped battling anxiety, it lost its power over me. (n.d.). *Everyday Mindfulness*. Retrieved from https://www.everyday-mindfulness.org/once-i-stopped-battling-anxiety-it-lost-its-power-over-me/

Resilience: Build skills to endure hardship. (n.d.). *Mayo Clinic*. Retrieved from https://www.mayoclinic.org/tests-procedures/resilience-training/in-depth/resilience/art-20046311

Self-validation: DBT skills, worksheets, videos, exercises. (n.d.). *Dialectical Behavior Therapy*. Retrieved from https://dialecticalbehaviortherapy.com/emotion-regulation/self-validation/

Symptoms of daughters of narcissistic mothers. (n.d.). *Charlie Health*. Retrieved from https://www.charliehealth.com/post/10-symptoms-of-daughters-of-narcissistic-mothers#:~:text=Daughters%20of%20narcissistic%20mothers%20often%20struggle%20with%20low%20self%2Desteem,being%20overly%20critical%20of%20oneself.

The impact of 'scapegoat' and 'golden child' dynamics. (n.d.). *Thrive Counseling Solutions*. Retrieved from https://www.thrivecounsellingsolutions.com/post/the-golden-child-and-the-scapegoat-dynamic-explained#:~:text=How

%20Do%20These%20Roles%20Impact,jealousy%2C%20and%20misunderstanding%20between%20siblings.

The impact of growing up with a narcissistic parent. (n.d.). *Heather Hayes & Associates*. Retrieved from https://heatherhayes.com/the-impact-of-growing-up-with-a-narcissistic-parent/

The psychological cost of never saying no. (n.d.). *Harley Therapy*. Retrieved from https://www.harleytherapy.co.uk/counselling/saying-no.htm

Toxic family members: How to maintain boundaries. (n.d.). *Savant Care*. Retrieved from https://www.savantcare.com/blog/toxic-family-members-how-to-maintain-boundaries/

Will the drama ever end? - *Will I Ever Be Good Enough?* (n.d.). Retrieved from https://willieverbegoodenough.com/will-the-drama-ever-end/

Made in the USA
Middletown, DE
08 July 2025